T0313437

Praise for *Small Stocks, Big Money*

"If you want a focused read on how to get rich buying smaller-cap stocks, this is the book. Mr. Gentry is at the top of his game. He writes with ease and grace as he describes how the big men got rich in microcaps."

—*Ray Akers, executive chairman, Akers BioSciences, NASDAQ: AKER*

"*Small Stocks, Big Money* is a fascinating read. It gives a solid account of the psyche, discipline, and the value systems of some of today's most successful microcap investors. This book is a must-read for both investors and entrepreneurs who are developing or investing in growth companies."

—*Dhru Desai, executive chairman, Quadrant 4 Systems*

"*Small Stocks, Big Money* is the comprehensive guide to navigating the sporty world of smaller-cap investing. You'll enjoy learning about how men like Byron Roth built an investment banking powerhouse in Southern California finding small companies that later became dominant players in their space."

—*Dan Erdberg, chief operating officer, Drone Aviation Corp.*

"Gentry has delivered what has never been done until now, providing a detailed picture of the microcap landscape with all its twists and turns, winners and losers. This is a book long overdue. *Small Stocks, Big Money* is chock full of wisdom from some of the best players in the business. It belongs on the desk of every investor who wants to learn from the pros how to make money investing in microcap stocks."

—*Paul Burgess, CEO and president, Lattice, Inc.*

"*Small Stocks, Big Money* should be mandatory reading for anyone studying business or finance. As a long-time owner of a small-cap investment bank, I was pleased to discover a book that provides a sweeping history of the microcap space. This is a book that every stock broker and every banker in the country could benefit from reading."

—Richard Rappaport, founder and CEO, WestPark Capital

"Dave Gentry is a rare find in the microcap space. As the CEO of a public company, I found *Small Stocks, Big Money* an incredibly helpful guide. If you want to know how to make it in this space, this is your book. It's a great read for novices and professionals."

—George C. Carpenter IV, CEO and president, CNS Response, Inc.

"Dave Gentry has my respect and admiration. As a CEO new to the microcap space, I am quite pleased to know that I am working with a team that knows the ins and outs of smaller-cap stocks. *Small Stocks, Big Money* is a sizzling look at those who dominate this volatile world. It's a fascinating read."

—Andrew Durgee, CEO, The Cointree

"*Small Stocks, Big Money* is a unique and privileged look at the ultra-rich in microcaps. This book is a great read on two counts: lots of practical business advice, and it serves as a basic tutorial on how to make millions buying small growth stocks."

—John Lorenz, CEO, Global Recycling Technologies

"*Small Stocks, Big Money* is a study in how the biggest players in the microcap space became rich but it also provides a historical context for both the Superstars and the companies they invested in, which make the book even more interesting."

—Richard Kreger, senior managing director of investment banking, Source Capital Group

Quotes from the Experts

"The single most important way we attempt to manage risk, in any environment, is by seeking to buy stocks very cheaply—we never want to pay too much."

—Bill Hench, portfolio manager, Royce Opportunity Funds,
Microcap Superstar

"Small caps outperform not because of market capitalization alone but because the stocks in this category are least efficiently priced."

—James O'Shaughnessy, author of What Works on Wall Street

"Higher returns, of course, come with more risk . . . the trade-off is, yes, you get long-term outperformance . . . but the volatility of returns is greater. . . . That's the price you pay if you want exposure to a better-performing asset class."

—Samuel Dedio, manager of the Artio U.S. Microcap Fund (JMCAX)

"The hardest part of raising capital for CPI was that we were totally unknown. I was a young Puerto Rican kid in Minneapolis, a land of Midwesterners. I had no previous history in manufacturing or inventing anything. Imagine you go to an investor and say, 'We're going to make a better pacemaker,' and they say, 'Doesn't Medtronic make a pacemaker?'"

—Manny Villafana, founder of St. Jude Medical, Inc.,
Microcap Superstar

"The risk always lies within management, so we're constantly evaluating through our three-part process. We meet with three to five CEOs and CFOs of small companies in our offices every week."

—Michael Corbett, manager, Perritt Capital Management,
Microcap Superstar

"We've found that the area that we can perform the best is in the microcap space. So it's a microcap value bent that really differentiates us, and that is because it's an area of the market where there are enormous inefficiencies and where our hard work pays off, because we can identify opportunities that are significantly underpriced."

—*Eric Kuby, chief investment officer,*
North Star Investment Management

"Investing in small- and microcap stocks requires significant time and resources because few investors are focused on the space. The reason that many investors do not pay attention to this space is that as managers' assets grow, it becomes increasingly difficult and cumbersome to allocate capital to less liquid and under-researched companies. With a higher level of assets under management, the contour of their portfolio, at some point, needs to change: either more names need to be included in the portfolio, diluting the impact of any single idea, or larger companies need to be included, forcing the portfolio to drift into a more efficiently priced universe."

Punch & Associates Investment Management, Inc.

"Be patient when buying. It might take six months to accumulate a position; you should be in for the long term and remember 20% of microcaps go to 0."

—*Buzz Heidkte, chairman, Midsouth Investors,*
Microcap Superstar

"Work hard, be a long-term thinker, develop tenacity and remember nothing happens without taking calculated risks."

—*Phil Sassower, chairman, Phoenix Group, Microcap Superstar*

"For me, the fun is to build, not to manage. I look for what's available, what is possible to do. That's the overriding consideration. There are a lot of things I would have liked to do, but didn't have the means."

—*Dr. Phil Frost, chairman, OPKO Health, Microcap Superstar*

"I've made my money by being the first in markets. As a venture capitalist, you have to seek out the cutting-edge companies. You get in as early as possible. That way you make a lot more headway and profits."

—*John Pappajohn, entrepreneur, philanthropist, business leader,*
Microcap Superstar

"Do your homework—understand companies you invest in forwards and backwards."

—Charles Diker, Diker Management, Microcap Superstar

"Investment advisors generally steer clients away from small stocks because they can be volatile and offer lower returns on average than their larger, more stable counterparts. Microcaps, then, are usually viewed as a trade to take advantage of momentary price movements, rather than as a long-term investment."

—Jeff Cox, finance editor, CNBC

"I had grown tired of backing make-believe CEOs and entrepreneurs, so my partners and I went on the board, took a hands-on approach, built the company, and put in a solid management team" (Interclick, sold to Yahoo! for $270 million).

—Barry Honig, founder, GRQ Consultants, Microcap Superstar

"Invest in something you can get your arms around and be very conservative, own enough stock so that you are not putting all your eggs in one basket."

—Dave Maley, fund manager, Ariel Microcap Funds,
Microcap Superstar

"If you want to invest in the microcap space, buy companies, not stocks; if you buy stocks, the daily fluctuations and lack of liquidity will drive you crazy."

—Byron Roth, CEO, ROTH Capital, Microcap Superstar

"Microcaps are a three-card-Monte play. If you don't know how to play, stay away."

—Greg Sichenzia, founding partner,
Sichenzia Ross Friedman Ference LLP,
Microcap Superstar

Small Stocks, Big Money

Small Stocks, Big Money

Interviews with Microcap Superstars

DAVE GENTRY

WILEY

Published by John Wiley & Sons, Inc., Hoboken, New Jersey.
Published simultaneously in Canada.

Library of Congress Cataloging-in-Publication Data:

Gentry, Dave, 1959—author.
  Small stocks, big money : interviews with microcap superstars / Dave Gentry.
    pages cm
  Includes indexes.
  ISBN 978-1-119-17255-0 (cloth); ISBN 978-1-119-17258-1 (ePDF);
  ISBN 978-1-11-917257-4 (ePub)
  1. Small capitalization stocks. 2. Portfolio management. 3. Speculation.
4. Investment advisors—Case studies. I. Title.
  HG4971.G46 2016
  332.63'22—dc23
                                                        2015029219

10 9 8 7 6 5 4 3 2 1

To Clare

The market is not simply a digital machine executing trades, reflecting buy and sell orders, and recording price movements. The market does not operate as an island unto itself. The market is an extension of the investors who bring it to life every day, investors who breathe into it all their prejudices, presuppositions, knowledge and lack of knowledge, needs, hopes, and fears, rational and irrational. Apply this truth to the microcap asset class and we are left with volatility and inefficiencies extraordinaire.

—Dave Gentry

Disclaimer

*L*imit of liability/disclaimer of warranty: The publisher and the author make no representations or warranties with respect to the accuracy or completeness of the contents of this work and specifically disclaim all warranties, including without limitation warranties of fitness for a particular purpose. The material in this book is for information purposes only and is not an offer to sell or the solicitation of an offer to buy any stocks mentioned herein. Additionally, the material contained herein is not a personal recommendation for any particular investor or client and does not take into account the financial, investment, or other objectives or needs of, and may not be suitable for, any particular investor or investment. If professional assistance is required, the services of a competent professional person should be sought. Neither the publisher nor the author shall be liable for damages arising herefrom. RedChip companies and Dave Gentry personally may hold positions in RedChip client companies and may buy or sell the securities at the same time investors are buying and selling.

Contents

Preface

The men you will meet in this book have spent much of their careers investing in smaller-cap companies. They have endured the test of time, making millions and in some cases hundreds of millions, through hard work, integrity, and a great capacity for risk, and perhaps, most important, the smarts to seize opportunities before others see them.

A college professor once reminded me that great things often happen in small places. The airplane was not invented at Harvard or MIT; it was invented by two brothers from Millville, Indiana, in Kitty Hawk, North Carolina. Starbucks was founded in 1971 in Seattle, Washington, as a small store selling roasted whole coffee beans. Apple started in a garage in 1976 selling computer kits, initially funded with a $10,000 investment. Caremark, the first home healthcare company, was a spin-off of a struggling biotech company that was funded by John Pappajohn, the Greek tycoon and Microcap Superstar.

Interclick, an Internet advertising company, was the brain child of Barry Honig, the most prolific microcap player today. In 2008 it was a $2.00 stock. A few years later, Yahoo! bought the company for $270 million. Subway started as a small sandwich shop in Bridgeport, Connecticut, 49 years ago with a $1,000 investment. Today, Subway has 39,500 franchises and generates $9.05 billion in annual sales. Phil Frost, the wealthiest Microcap Superstar, purchased a small company struggling to make payroll called Key Pharmaceuticals, in 1972. Fourteen years later he sold it to Schering-Plough for $800 million. Big companies start small.

Cardiac Pacemakers, founded in January 1972 by Microcap Superstar Manny Villafana, went public as a pink-sheet, over-the-counter stock, raising $450,000 on May 26, 1972. Six years later, Eli Lilly (NYSE: LLY) purchased the company for $127 million. They later spun it out under the name Guidant, which was purchased by Boston Scientific in 2006 for $24.6 billion.

Most of the men in this book I have known personally. Those I have not, I either met for the interview for this book, or learned about from my own research or through close friends or colleagues who know them well. This is by no means an exhaustive list of the Superstars in microcaps. There are others who deserve to be on this list whom I simply do not know, or whom I have not interviewed, and a few whom I know well, but who wish to continue their careers in relative anonymity.

The men you will meet in this book have spent much of their careers investing in smaller-cap companies. They have endured the test of time, making millions, and in some cases hundreds of millions, through hard work, integrity, and a great capacity for risk, and perhaps most important, the smarts to seize opportunities before others see them. None of the men in this book have been successful on every deal. Not every stock they have invested in, funded, started, or transacted business for has succeeded. In fact, some of the companies they were involved with have been miserable failures.

But they are all experts in the microcap space; all have something to teach us about investing in smaller-cap companies. These men are the crème de la crème of Wall Street's small stock community. They can go head-to-head with the best and brightest at the biggest research and investment banking firms on Wall Street. What is interesting about this group of individuals is they did not necessarily make a conscious decision to build careers in this asset class. It was much more likely that they found themselves early in their careers and, in some cases, as earlier as high school, around mentors who helped endear them to the world of smaller-cap stocks.

Michael Corbett, for example, who manages three funds for Perritt Capital Management, was mentored by Dr. Perritt, who was a professor of finance at DePaul University in the 1980s. He would take classes from him, and after getting his MBA go to work for him as an analyst. He now owns the funds he manages.

Barry Honig, mentored by his father, a successful Wall Street entrepreneur, started reading the *Wall Street Journal* while he was in high school, and after starting his career as a trader realized he could make more money buying and selling and investing in small stocks.

David Maley went to college thinking he would be a doctor or an engineer, but then he took a class called Investments, and then another called Advanced Investments, both taught by Sarkis Joseph Khoury, PhD, a prominent economist whose focus is international finance, mergers and acquisitions, debt restructuring, and speculative markets. Taking these classes changed David's thinking about what he wanted to do with his life. In 1981, while in his junior year at the University of Notre Dame, he changed his major to business.

I want to note that I am not an analyst, nor have I ever been a stock broker, fund manager, or registered investment advisor. I am an entrepreneur who has spent the past 15 years working the microcap street, most of it as the president and owner of RedChip Companies, an investor relations, media, and research firm focused on smaller-cap companies. I will be the first to admit that I have made my share of mistakes in this business. There are companies that I believed in with strong conviction that failed; there are many that have yet to live up to my expectations. I have represented more than 400 public companies over the past 18 years. I have badly misjudged management teams, grossly overvalued the prospects of companies, and missed seeing red flags that I should have. I have also been conned a few times by CEOs who were simply disingenuous in their representations of their companies. Through it all, I continue to learn and grow.

☆ ☆ ☆

All of the men in this book I consider self-made, though some enjoyed the benefit and inherent advantage of Ivy League educations, such as Phil Sassower, Charles Diker, and Phil Frost. Indeed, we can learn a great deal from these men about how to make money investing in microcaps. We can also learn from their application of timeless principles of success: the importance of a strong work ethic, the importance of continuous education, and daily habits that lead to success, like getting up at 4:30 a.m. every day and reading the financial papers, as John Pappajohn, one of the all-time greats in the microcap space, has done for 55 years.

Acknowledgments

I want to thank first and foremost my wife, Clare, for giving me the time and space to write, think, and reflect over the past 12 months as I worked on this book. She has been gracious and supportive in so many ways. Second, I want to thank the RedChip team, particularly Thomas Pfister, my research director, Paul Kuntz, my communications director, and Alan Bracamonte, who spent long hours designing and laying out the book. I would also like to thank all of the Superstars in this book for lending me their time to learn about their remarkable stories.

PART I

Big Companies Start Small

CHAPTER 1

Microcap Stocks, the Neglected Asset Class

Considering the fact that almost 50% of the approximately 16,000 public companies (this number includes OTC market stocks) in the United States have market caps of under $500 million, the lack of research and media coverage on this sector is surprising.

U.S. Public Companies' Market Caps
- 7,360 under $500 million
- 6,622 under $250 million
- 5,713 under $100 million
- 5,053 under $50 million

—Thomson Reuters, September 7, 2014

The microcap sector is one of the least-understood asset classes on Wall Street. It is also the most neglected sector by the major financial media outlets. CNBC, Fox Business, and Bloomberg offer precious little content or commentary on microcap stocks. Fox Business's Charles Payne is the only mainstream Wall Street media pundit who has experience in the sector. Jim Cramer, on his show *Mad Money*, does occasionally comment on microcap companies (in fact, he has mentioned several RedChip client companies over the years), but he is largely focused on large and mid-caps. My show, *Small Stocks, Big Money*, is the only show approved by major networks (Fox Business, Bloomberg Europe, Bloomberg Asia) that focuses exclusively on microcap stocks, and at this point we still have to pay for our air time.

It is not often that we see the major business media outlets discussing, providing commentary, or interviewing the rainmakers in the U.S smaller-cap sector. Rarely do we see interviews with the CEOs of public companies with market caps under $250 million, though there are plenty of fast-growing, profitable companies from which to choose, some of which you will read about in this book.

> What the mainstream financial pundits forget is that big companies generally start small. In my debate with Herb Greenberg, Gary Kaminsky, and David Faber on CNBC in November 2011, related to reverse merger Chinese small-cap stocks, I tried to make the point that Blockbuster Video, Texas Instruments (NASDAQ: TXN), and even the New York Stock Exchange (NYSE: ICE), went public through the reverse merger process, an alternative to IPOs used by many small companies.

A *reverse merger* is an inexpensive way of going public that circumvents the IPO process and the associated costs. This alternative listing mechanism is used today by many start-ups and less developed companies.

Greenberg and others also betrayed their lack of knowledge of the microcap sector when they questioned whether institutions purchased small and microcap stocks covered by RedChip analysts when in fact hundreds of institutions meet with the CEOs of RedChip companies every year, many of whom build large positions in our stocks. Not only did they cut me off seven times in a 15-minute discussion, they implicitly disparaged the entire microcap asset class over and over again. Their show, called *The Strategy Session*, was later canceled.

Over the past 24 months, NASDAQ OMX Group and the NYSE: MKT has listed dozens of "small" companies that went public through the reverse merger process on the OTC markets, which is the home of thousands of smaller companies intent on listing on a major exchange. Another problem with the sector is that there are simply not enough independent analysts covering microcap stocks. There is a plethora of issuer-sponsored research, some of it quite good, but because it is paid for by the issuer, in some circles it is not given the respect that it deserves. The investment banks who focus on smaller-cap companies, with few exceptions, save their research for companies they back.

Considering the fact that almost 50% of the approximately 16,000 public companies (this number includes OTC market stocks) in the United States have market caps of under $500 million, the lack of research and media coverage on this sector is surprising. Michael Corbett, CEO of Perritt Capital Management, summed the issue up well when he explained that it is much easier for analysts and the pundits to talk about the big companies because there is so much history and information. Also, the white-shoe firms such as Goldman Sachs and JP Morgan learned a long time ago that because smaller stocks lack the liquidity of the larger names, it's harder to generate substantial fees trading these stocks. So it's best to stick with the big and midcaps where the fees are bigger and the information is better.

Sometimes big companies with long track records lose market cap due to a lack of execution, innovation, or poor financial management, and fall back into the microcap category. Superstar Phil Sassower invested in New Park Resources (NYSE: NR) in 1986 at 20 cents a share after it was delisted from the NYSE. He revitalized the company with new money and management, refocused the business, and made an enormous profit on his investment.

> You will hear over and over again in this book from the Superstars that management is the most important factor to consider when investing in small, lesser known companies. It does not follow logically that great technology or a great idea translates into a successful company.

Jim Collins's epic study of great companies in *Good to Great* teaches us that the first and most important thing a company must do to get better or to become great is to *get the right people on the bus* and *get the wrong people off the bus*. If this is true for big companies, then it is extraordinarily true for microcaps.

Collins's study looked at over 1,400 companies and found only 11 that made the transition from good to great, defined by outperforming the market by at least three times over a 15-year period. If less than 1% of those big companies made the transition from *good to great,* then one can imagine how few microcaps make the transition from *bad to better, okay to good,* or *good to great.*

Buying microcaps when they are least efficient, before the truth about the company is fully known by the Street, is how investors can maximize their returns. And this is what the Superstars have been able to do consistently. Inside this book you will find dozens of examples of how the Superstars invested in companies, many times when no one else would, because they had the acumen and the foresight to understand what others missed, a technology, product, or service that with the right capitalization, management, or marketing could become successful.

Barry Honig and Phil Frost invested in MusclePharm (OTCQB: MSLP), when it was a subpenny stock and hemorrhaging losses. They restructured the company, did a reverse split, and led a $10 million capital raise. What they saw was a company with industry-leading muscle-enhancing nutritional products and a very large market opportunity. Eighteen months after their investment, the stock traded at a $175 million market cap. The stock has

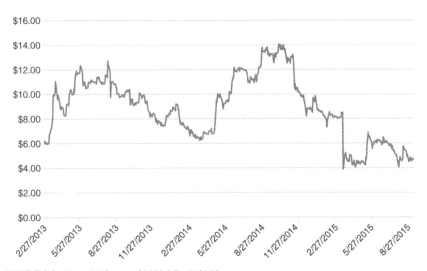

FIGURE 1.1 MusclePharm (OTCQB: MSLP)
Data Source: Thomson Reuters Corporation.

since fallen to a $64 million market cap. In 2014, the company generated
$177 million in revenue, with a loss of $13 million. For the first six months
of 2015, it reported revenue of $91 million and losses of $14.5 million (see
Figure 1.1).

Every stock has a life cycle. Every stock has its proverbial ups and
downs. But the life cycles of microcap stocks are different, more erratic,
and more volatile. They tend to move up faster but can also fall faster.
Some trade in familiar patterns, up two to three points like clockwork
only to fall back down two to three points the next day, week, or
month. Indeed, the microcap world can be fast and furious. There are
momentum plays every day of the trading year with daily and weekly
price swings of 10% to 100%+.

The neglected asset class is full of opportunities for large gains, but is
also fraught with risk. The chart of Galectin Therapeutics (NASDAQ: GALT)
in Figure 1.2 tells a fascinating story. The stock closed at $8.08 December
31, 2013. Just 10 days later it closed at $15.10, an 87% gain in two weeks. It
pulled back to $11.59 on January 24, 2014, then burst to $18.30 on February
27, 2014. Less than three months later it was back at $10.28 but then gained
42 percent over the next seven weeks.

FIGURE 1.2 Galectin Therapeutics (NASDAQ: GALT)
Data Source: Thomson Reuters Corporation.

On July 25, the stock closed at $15.32. Four days later the stock lost 66% of its value when healthcare analyst Adam Feuerstein published a scathing article on TheStreet.com about the company. The critique was prompted by a July 24 article published by a firm paid by Galectin to promote their stock. In the July 24 article, the paid promoter stated that Galectin was "nipping at Intercept's heels," with a Phase I drug that treats NASH, nonalcoholic steatohepatitis (a form of fatty liver disease). Comparing Galectin, which was still in a Phase I trial, with a $4.5 billion market cap company that had already completed a Phase II clinical trial for a similar drug with positive data, Feuerstein argued was misleading and unethical. Feuerstein also questioned the efficacy of the endpoints of Galectin's Phase I trial. Galectin promptly responded with a press release defending their development program for GR-MD-02 (their drug for the treatment of NASH), potentially allaying concerns about their technology. The bigger issue uncovered was that insiders had sold 700,000 shares of stock "in the last twelve months."[1]

The question begs itself: Was the stock trading efficiently between $12.00 and $15.00 with a market cap of $300–$350 million, or was it now fairly valued at a $100 million market cap trading at $5.00? Nothing had changed about the company or its technology from July 25 to July 29. But in one day it lost 66% of its market cap. What did change is information that was already public regarding the insider selling of 700,000 shares over the past 12 months was brought to the attention of investors who were unaware of this fact. The insider selling, combined with what appeared to be a company-sponsored promotional campaign of their stock by promoters who appeared to be making exaggerated claims about the prospects of their lead drug, resulted in a massive selloff.

The fact is the results of their Phase I trial and the technology behind it were well known on the Street. Institutions such as BlackRock, BNY Mellon Asset Management, and dozens of other sophisticated investment management firms were positioned in the stock and still are today. Institutional holdings after this "new" information came to light only dropped 2.7%, quarter-over-quarter. The selloff appeared to be mostly from retail investors, who either did not know or had not thought much about the insider selling.

> When a microcap stock has a small number of tradeable shares (float), the stock can make lightning-fast moves up or down. These stocks can make extraordinary runs in a matter of days, becoming tremendously overvalued, based on a well-placed blog, or positive industry article, or news of a big contract, only to come crashing down a few days or a few weeks later as more information about the company comes to market.

These erratic runs sometimes look like pump-and-dumps, but that does not mean the company is a fraud or misleading investors, though that is sometimes the case. It often means that someone or some group of investors hold cheap stock, often the previous owners of the shell company if it was a reverse merger. Drone Aviation (OTCQB: DRNE) is one such example. Figure 1.3 is disturbing. The stock ran from $0.65 to $1.17 in just a few weeks after they began airing commercial spots on DirectTV financial stations and other media outlets.

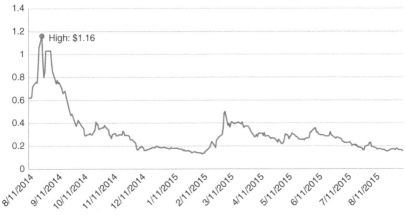

FIGURE 1.3 Drone Aviation Holding Corp. (OTC: DRNE)
Data Source: Thomson Reuters Corporation.

The 30-second TV commercial was factually accurate and was very effective in getting investors excited about the company. The stock went from trading 5,000 shares a day to trading hundreds of thousands of shares a day. But within four weeks after the run-up, it came crashing down to $0.30. The precipitous fall was due partly to a negative article written by a blogger who had little knowledge of the company or its technology, but who believed that with less than $5 million in sales, the stock did not deserve a $200 million market cap. Even though Dr. Phil Frost invested in the company, probably the savviest and by far the richest Microcap Superstar, this did not stop other bloggers from piling on with negative and for the most part factually incorrect blogs, which further helped drive the stock down. What was also true, however, is that there were a group of investors who held very cheap stock in Drone Aviation and many of them sold on the way up and on the way down. Hence, it looked like a proverbial pump-and-dump. Depending on where one bought and sold along the price continuum, and whether he was in for a short-term price swing or long-term gain, determines a lot about the state of mind of the investor after the stock lost 66% of its value. Those who did their homework realized that the precipitous price deterioration of Drone Aviation, like Galectin Therapeutics, created an excellent opportunity to accumulate.

Companies can be fundamentally sound and executing well, and still lose millions in market cap value for various reasons, including the filing of an S-1 or S-3 registration statement to prepare for a future capital raise. Investors fear dilution and exit, or short the stock, while potential new investors wait for the capital raise before positioning, and thus, the stock tumbles. Bill Hench of The Royce Funds says that he tries to buy stocks as cheaply as possible, but he does not try to time the market or his buys. The Royce Funds position for the long term and have billions under management. They can afford to wait two or three years for a stock to work out, but the individual investor often cannot. Thus, it is important to be prepared for the downside. The neglected asset class is also chock full of opportunities to lose. Lessons from the Superstars hopefully can help investors better understand and navigate the microcap landscape.

Note

1. Seeking Alpha, "Why This Penny Stock Dressed Up by Stock Promoters Is a Short," July 28, 2014.

PART II

The Superstars

CHAPTER 2

Michael Corbett

The most important lesson I've learned working in the microcap space is that winners are winners and losers are losers. Stick with the ones that are working, and don't make the mistake of exiting too early.

—Michael Corbett, Perritt Capital Management

Occupation: Majority Owner, Perritt Capital Management

Money Under Management: $650 million

Age: 50

Education: BSc in Finance and Accounting, DePaul University

Estimated Net Worth: $10 million

Status: Married, three children

Large Positions: John B. Sanfilippo & Son (NASDAQ: JBSS), Addus HomeCare (NASDAQ: ADUS)

Favorite Industries: Industrials, Technology, and Financials

Favorite Financial Books: *The Intelligent Investor*, Benjamin Graham; *Beating the Street*, Peter Lynch; *Learn to Earn*, Peter Lynch

Unlike many in the Superstar club, Michael Corbett did not grow up in a family of businessmen. His father was a steelworker, and like John Pappajohn, his dad died when he was young. After earning a BSc in Finance and Accounting at DePaul University, his first job out of college was as a gofer working for Charles Schwab. The plan was to get some basic training in the financial markets, then acquire his Series 7 license, but that plan was put on hold when the firm terminated him shortly after Black Monday (the October 19, 1987, market crash). Ultimately, 15,000 Wall Street professionals lost their jobs that year.

Only 24 years old at the time of the crash, Corbett began working for Dr. Gerald W. Perritt, who taught Business Administration at DePaul University and was also the founder of Perritt Capital Management. He was also the first executive director of the American Association of Individual Investors, a *Forbes* columnist, and the author of several books, including *The Mutual Fund Encyclopedia* and *Small Stocks, Big Profits*.

Perritt gave him a job researching stocks for his small-cap newsletter. After five years of researching and writing for the newsletter, he moved to the money management side of the business and eventually became the portfolio manager of the firm. In 2010, he purchased the firm from Perritt and became its CEO and CIO. He manages three microcap funds with total assets of $600 million. He invests in companies with market caps as low as $5 million and as high as $500 million. He currently favors industrial and energy stocks.

Perritt's Investment Paradigm

The firm's investment paradigm relies on the work of a former University of Chicago accounting professor named Joseph Piotroski, who now is a professor at Stanford's Graduate School of Business. In 2000, Dr. Piotroski published a paper, "Value Investing: The Use of Financial Statement Information to Separate Winners from Losers,"[1] which received widespread attention among Wall Street professionals and the financial media. The starting point for his analysis is finding companies whose "book/market ratios (the inverse of the price/book ratio) are in the top 20% of the market." He then evaluates them using fundamental analysis looking at such metrics as return on assets rate, current ratio, and change in gross margins. His research showed that if his formula was applied between 1976 and 1996, which meant buying the top stocks and shorting the worst of those screened, the annualized return would have been 23%, considerably better than the S&P 500 during the same period.

> Corbett's analysis starts with ranking all companies by market cap, separating the bottom 20% of companies from the top 80% of companies, and then using a nine-criteria screening process.

The stock can earn one point or zero points for each of the nine criteria, he explains. A 20-year research effort by Piotroski showed that if investors chose for their portfolios only those "value" stocks that scored eight or nine points as opposed to a portfolio of all value stocks, the portfolio with only eight or nine scores outperformed the other portfolio by 7.5% annually.

The Nine Investment Criteria

1. Net Income: Bottom line. Score 1 if last-year net income is positive.
2. Operating Cash Flow: A better earnings gauge. Score 1 if last-year cash flow is positive.
3. Return on Assets: Measures profitability. Score 1 if last-year ROA exceeds prior-year ROA.
4. Quality of Earnings: Warns of accounting tricks. Score 1 if last-year operating cash flow exceeds net income.
5. Long-Term Debt versus Assets: Is debt decreasing? Score 1 if the ratio of long-term debt to assets is down from the year-ago value. (If LTD is zero but assets are increasing, score 1 anyway.)
6. Current Ratio: Measures increasing working capital. Score 1 if CR has increased from the prior year.
7. Shares Outstanding: A measure of potential dilution. Score 1 if the number of shares outstanding is no greater than the year-ago figure.
8. Gross Margin: A measure of improving competitive position. Score 1 if full-year GM exceeds the prior-year GM.
9. Asset Turnover: Measures productivity. Score 1 if the percentage increase in sales exceeds the percentage increase in total assets.

After evaluating the company based on these quantitative criteria (only those stocks with scores between 6 and 9 make it into the second round), the second round of analysis is qualitative, which involves a close analysis of management, and a proper understanding of the company's product or service and its competitive position in the marketplace. He notes that with the Ultra-Microcap fund he is more flexible in the nine-point test. But one area in which he is not flexible is the quality of management.

> "I like management to own a lot of stock and I like to see them buying in the open market. I also look closely at their long-term track record to determine their strengths and/or weaknesses," Piotroski says.

In essence, from a quantitative standpoint, he is looking for stocks with growth at a reasonable price (GARP), or what are also known as value stocks. If the company cannot be evaluated on GARP criteria, such as a cyclical stock like a car manufacturer or airline, which tend to perform better during a time when the economy is fundamentally strong, then he may look at a price-to-sales or price-to-earnings metric as part of the evaluation process. He generally gives a stock about three years to work.

Corbett explains, "The most important lesson I've learned working in the microcap space is that winners are winners and losers are losers. Stick with the ones that are working, and don't make the mistake of exiting too early."

I will note here that Corbett's ultra-microcap fund invested $1 million in a current RedChip client company, Quadrant 4 Systems (OTCQB: QFOR), a fast-growing Chicago-based IT company with a unique healthcare exchange platform technology. He bought the stock in a private placement at $0.30 in 2010 and added to his position at $0.35 in 2011. The stock retraced to $0.03 in early 2013 and was $0.06 cents on the day the company signed a 12-month investor relations contract with RedChip in August 2013 (Figure 2.1). I asked him why he bought Quadrant 4 initially, and also why he did not sell when the stock depreciated so dramatically.

"The QFOR position was an outlier for us," he said, "but I liked management. I like Dhru Desai (executive chairman). I believed they had the vision and the right team to execute on their plan. With small companies it's all about management."

On the issue of why he did not sell when the stock plummeted, he explained: "If we are losing more than 50%, we ask ourselves, 'Are we missing something?' We called the CEO and asked him why we shouldn't walk

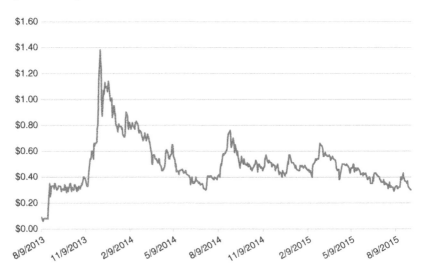

FIGURE 2.1 Quadrant 4 Systems (OTCQB: QFOR)
Data Source: Thomson-Reuters Corporation.

away. They kept calling back, answering our questions, allaying our concerns. They were honest and upfront. We appreciated that. Unlike some management teams, they never tried to hide anything from us and they kept calling us back."

> In comparing microcaps to larger cap stocks, Corbett explains that "over the long-term, it is the best place for exposure to equities with the opportunity for the biggest returns, but be prepared for extreme volatility and get in for the long term. Some situations take a while to develop. If after three years the stock is not working, if it is not getting respect, there is probably a good reason for it."

One stock he laments not holding longer is Middleby (NASDAQ: MIDD), a global leader in the foodservice equipment industry. Founded in 1985, the company was the successor to the Middleby Marshall Company, a maker of high-quality, commercial conveyor ovens used by major pizza chains such as Domino's. They generated sales of $25 million in 1986, losing $1.1 million.[2]

The company uplisted from the OTC Bulletin Board in 1988 to the American Stock Exchange (AMEX). The company grew significantly throughout the 1990s, primarily by making strategic acquisitions and expanding internationally. Though encumbered with a heavy debt load, which they refinanced several times, by 2000, they were experiencing the benefits of several key acquisitions and the expansion of their product line internationally. The Company would later list on the NASDAQ and become wildly successful, emerging as a world leader in foodservice equipment. In 2013, they reported revenue of $1.4 billion and earnings of $153.9 million. He started buying the stock in late 2003, split adjusted at around $20 a share, when it had a $150 million market cap. By October 2014, the market cap was $5.1 billion (Figure 2.2).

If there is a lesson in this story that we see over and over again in this book, it is that companies that appear mediocre can emerge from small, struggling enterprises into giants of their industries and provide huge returns for patient investors. Middleby possessed four qualities that contributed to their remarkable 29-year run:

1. An industry-best patented technology that provided a strong foundation for their early years.
2. A very large and growing market opportunity for their products. Foodservice sales were $213 billion in 1988 and reached $661 billion in 2013 (National Restaurant Association).

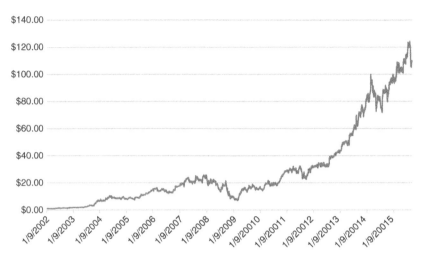

FIGURE 2.2 Middleby Corporation (NASDAQ: MIDD)
Data Source: Thomson-Reuters Corporation.

3. A strong, focused, and disciplined leadership team of industry veterans.
4. Competent investment banking partners along the way who believed in their product and management team.

"I wish I had held every share that I bought from the beginning, but I didn't. I left too early and left a lot of money on the table," Corbett says.

> If one had purchased 10,000 shares of Middleby (NASDAQ: MIDD) on March 7, 2000, roughly a $31,900 investment, that investment would be worth $2,852,000 today.

One stock that he has let run is Virtus Investment Partners, Inc. (NASDAQ: VRTS), a money management firm that runs several mutual funds, based in Hartford, CT. This company was formed in 1995 through a reverse merger with Duff & Phelps Investment Management Co. A *reverse merger* is an alternative method of going public that is quicker and less expensive than a traditional IPO and is used by many microcap companies as a starting point to go public. Though much maligned by the mainstream financial media, many very successful companies have used this process to go public, including the New York Stock Exchange (NYSE: ICE).

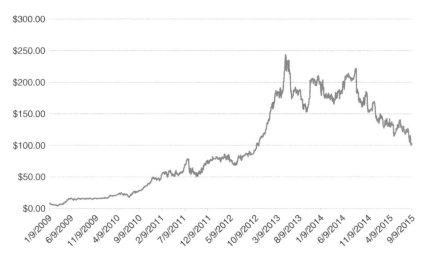

FIGURE 2.3 Virtus Investment Partners, Inc. (NASDAQ: VRTS)
Data Source: Thomson-Reuters Corporation.

Corbett began buying Virtus in 2010, when the market cap was $100 million and the stock was trading between $13 and $18 per share. The market cap of Virtus reached $1.5 billion and traded at $168.00 per share in October 2014. The stock is currently trading at $102 per share with a market cap of $907 million (as of September 8, 2015) (Figure 2.3).

"When we discovered Virtus, no one was buying the stock, no one knew about it. They had $20 billion under management and $30 million cash in the bank. They now have $40 billion under management and their earnings numbers have exploded," Corbett explains.

Corbett believes investors should be looking closely at Energy, Industrial, and Technology stocks. He believes that energy issues will continue to play a major role in world and domestic affairs.

Today, Corbett's favorite energy service company is Newpark Resources (NYSE: NR), an oil and gas company providing products and services to the oil and gas industry. Among other services, the company has a fleet of helicopters that deliver equipment to oil rigs. He also likes Manitex International (NASDAQ: MNTX). This company markets boom trucks and sign, sky, and truck cranes and other engineered lifting solutions. On March 6, 2014, they announced record revenue of $245.1 million, up 19% from the previous year, and net income of $10.2 million, up 26% from the prior year. In 2010 the stock traded below $2.00. The stock closed on March 6, 2014, at $15.99.

The Perritt Low-Priced Stock Fund was named a Category King by the *Wall Street Journal* for June 30, 2015, among Small Cap Core Funds based on Lipper data. The Category King award recognizes the top 10 funds in each category for one-year total returns.

Michael Corbett's approach to investing is disciplined and focused. He uses a strict quantitative analysis but also looks at qualitative factors that make room for stocks that do not score perfectly on his quantitative scale. Three important lessons emerge from Corbett's approach to buying microcaps.

1. If you have an investment approach that is working, don't change it.
2. Once you have done your homework and chosen to invest in a company, be patient, give it time to work. He gives his investments three years to work.
3. Look for undervalued energy companies. Energy issues will continue to play a major role in world and domestic affairs.

Perritt Capital Management Top Stock Positions

Perritt Ultra MicroCap Mutual Fund

Company	Position (m)	% Fund Assets
Fidelity Instl Money Market Portfolio	3.08m	4.63%
Cherokee Inc. Ord	0.06m	2.62%
USA Technologies Inc. Ord	0.53m	2.15%
Juniper Pharmaceuticals Inc. Ord	0.15m	2.02%
Newtek Business Services Corp. Ord	0.07m	1.87%
Century Casinos Inc. Ord	0.18m	1.71%
Hill International Inc. Ord	0.20m	1.55%
Supreme Industries Inc. Ord	0.12m	1.55%
Hennessy Advisors Inc. Ord	0.05m	1.52%
DSP Group Inc. Ord	0.10m	1.52%
Atlas Financial Holdings Inc. Ord	0.05m	1.49%
Ballantyne Strong Inc. Ord	0.21m	1.47%
Kingstone Companies Inc. Ord	0.13m	1.46%
Globalscape Inc. Ord	0.29m	1.44%
John B. Sanfilippo & Son Inc. Ord	0.02m	1.41%
Pacific Premier Bancorp Inc. Ord	0.06m	1.40%
Willamette Valley Vineyards Inc. Ord	0.13m	1.39%
AXT Inc. Ord	0.35m	1.32%
Hurco Companies Inc. Ord	0.03m	1.30%
Q4 Systems Corp. Ord	1.98m	1.25%
Information Services Group Inc. Ord	0.17m	1.20%
Asure Software Inc. Ord	0.13m	1.16%
Hudson Technologies Inc. Ord	0.22m	1.16%
DHT Holdings Inc. Ord	0.10m	1.15%
DLH Holdings Corp. Ord	0.29m	1.14%
Addus Homecare Corp. Ord	0.03m	1.13%
Intest Corp. Ord	0.17m	1.13%

Company	Position (m)	% Fund Assets
Hackett Group Inc. Ord	0.05m	1.07%
Pioneer Power Solutions Inc. Ord	0.10m	1.06%
PCM Inc. Ord	0.07m	1.06%
Napco Security Technologies Inc. Ord	0.12m	1.04%
First Internet Bancorp Ord	0.03m	1.03%
Bsquare Corp. Ord	0.10m	1.02%
Gencor Industries Inc. Ord	0.07m	1.02%
Trinity Biotech Plc Dr.	0.04m	1.02%
Evolving Systems Inc. Ord	0.08m	1.01%
Auxilio Inc. Ord	0.63m	1.00%
CTI Industries Corp. Ord	0.18m	1.00%
Mobivity Hldgs Corp. Ord	0.66m	0.97%
Iteris Inc. Ord	0.36m	0.96%
TheStreet Inc. Ord	0.35m	0.95%
Willdan Group Inc. Ord	0.06m	0.95%
Xplore Technologies Corp. Ord	0.11m	0.93%
Data I/O Corp. Ord	0.18m	0.93%
Flexible Solutions International Inc. Ord	0.30m	0.93%
Birner Dental Management Services Inc. Ord	0.05m	0.92%
ADDvantage Technologies Group Inc. Ord	0.26m	0.90%
Metalico Inc. Ord	1.17m	0.90%
KVH Industries Inc. Ord	0.04m	0.89%
Hopfed Bancorp Inc. Ord	0.05m	0.89%
United Insurance Holdings Corp. Ord	0.04m	0.89%
Concurrent Computer Corp. Ord	0.10m	0.89%
Innodata Inc. Ord	0.22m	0.87%
Northern Technologies Int'l Corp. Ord	0.04m	0.87%
Digital Turbine Inc. Ord	0.19m	0.87%
Nevada Gold & Casinos Inc. Ord	0.35m	0.87%
iPass Inc. Ord	0.54m	0.85%
Orbit International Corp. Ord	0.19m	0.85%
Magicjack VocalTec Ltd. Ord	0.08m	0.84%
Edgewater Technology Inc. Ord	0.08m	0.82%
1347 Property Insurance Holdings Inc. Ord	0.07m	0.80%
Diversified Restaurant Holdings Inc. Ord	0.14m	0.79%
Ari Network Services Inc. Ord	0.16m	0.76%
Ultralife Corp. Ord	0.12m	0.76%
Transcat Inc. Ord	0.05m	0.74%
Intrusion Inc. Ord	0.26m	0.74%
Crown Crafts Inc. Ord	0.06m	0.74%
BG Staffing Inc. Ord	0.04m	0.73%

(Continued)

Company	Position (m)	% Fund Assets
Amrep Corp. Ord	0.10m	0.73%
Fitlife Brands Inc. Ord	0.28m	0.72%
Hardinge Inc. Ord	0.05m	0.67%
US Auto Parts Network Inc. Ord	0.20m	0.66%
LGI Homes Inc. Ord	0.02m	0.66%
Uranium Energy Corp. Ord	0.27m	0.65%
Professional Diversity Network Inc. Ord	0.20m	0.63%
Mitcham Industries Inc. Ord	0.10m	0.63%
Xenith Bankshares Inc. Ord	0.07m	0.62%
Kratos Defense and Security Solutions Inc. Ord	0.07m	0.62%
Richardson Electronics Ltd. Ord	0.05m	0.61%
Empire Resources Inc. Ord	0.10m	0.60%
RCM Technologies Inc. Ord	0.07m	0.60%
Liberty Tax Inc. Ord	0.02m	0.60%
Allied Motion Technologies Inc. Ord	0.02m	0.59%
Fuel Tech Inc. Ord	0.18m	0.59%
MeetMe Inc. Ord	0.23m	0.58%
Cyberoptics Corp. Ord	0.04m	0.58%
LifeVantage Corp. Ord	0.70m	0.56%
General Finance Corp. Ord	0.07m	0.55%
NV5 Holdings Inc. Ord	0.02m	0.55%
Tor Minerals International Inc. Ord	0.06m	0.54%
SmartPros Ltd .Ord	0.20m	0.54%
Dawson Geophysical Co .Ord	0.08m	0.53%
Gaming Partners International Corp. Ord	0.03m	0.50%
Hallador Energy Co. Ord	0.04m	0.50%
AG&E Holdings Inc. Ord	0.39m	0.49%
Air Industries Group Ord	0.03m	0.48%
Widepoint Corp. Ord	0.18m	0.45%
CPI Aerostructures Inc. Ord	0.03m	0.45%
Aerocentury Corp. Ord	0.03m	0.43%
Charles & Colvard Ltd. Ord	0.18m	0.40%
Hooper Holmes Inc. Ord	1.31m	0.38%
Galaxy Gaming Inc. Ord	1.53m	0.37%
Enservco Corp. Ord	0.14m	0.31%
Deep Down Inc. Ord	0.28m	0.31%
NTN Buzztime Inc. Ord	0.71m	0.25%
Tecnoglass Inc. Ord	0.01m	0.16%
ID Systems Inc. Ord	0.01m	0.08%
LGL Group EQY Warrant	0.25m	0.00%

Source: Thomson Reuters Corporation.

Notes

1. J. D. Piotroski, "Value Investing: The Use of Financial Statement Information to Separate Winners from Losers," *Journal of Accounting Research* 38, Supplement (2000): 1–41.
2. FundingUniverse, "The Middleby Corporation History," www.fundinguniverse.com/company-histories/the-middleby-corporation-history.

CHAPTER 3

Bill Hench

The single most important way we attempt to manage risk, in any environment, is by seeking to buy stocks very cheaply—we never want to pay too much.

—Bill Hench, The Royce Funds

Occupation: Portfolio Manager, Royce Funds

Co-Manages: Royce Opportunity Fund ($2.5 billion assets)

Manages: Royce Micro-Cap Opportunity Fund ($24 million assets)

Age: 50

Education: Bachelor degree in Accounting, Adelphi University, 1986

Estimated Net Worth: $10 million

Status: Married, three children

Residence: Manhattan, NY

Favorite Industry: Information Technology

Bill Hench says he is a reformed CPA. He received his degree in Accounting from Adelphi University in 1983 and began his career with Coopers & Lybrand. He then spent 10 years in the institutional equity business in Boston and New York, most recently with JP Morgan. For the past 10 years, he has been focused on smaller-cap companies at Royce Funds. He said he found microcaps much more interesting than big caps because of their greater inefficiencies and opportunities for bigger returns.

With over $30 billion under management across 15 funds, Royce is one of the largest family of funds in the world. He manages two of those funds, the Royce Opportunity Fund, which uses a broadly diversified portfolio, with a theme-based, opportunistic value approach focused exclusively on small-cap stocks with market caps of up to $2.5 billion. The fund's net asset value is $2.5 billion. He also manages the Royce Micro-Cap Opportunity Fund, which also uses a theme-based, opportunistic value approach with $24 million of net assets. Both of these funds are weighted heavily in Information Technology, Industrials, and Energy stocks.

The following is an interview I conducted with him for my TV show, *Small Stocks, Big Money*. For the sake of clarity, I have made some slight grammatical modifications to the text. (Interviewed October 9, 2014)

Dave: Bill, thanks for being with us today.

Bill: Thanks very much for having me.

Dave: You're a portfolio manager at one of the world's largest small-microcap funds. The Opportunity Fund and the Opportunity Select Fund are two that you work with, two of the ten or so that your firm manages. Now tell us about what you mean by your investment approach: opportunistic value and theme-based stocks.

Bill: Sure, so really what we're doing is trying to find stocks that are presenting themselves as really, really cheap at a given point in time, right? So what does that mean? They're cheap for a reason. They either had a bad earnings quarter or perhaps they had an inventory issue or a cost issue, thousands of things can happen that can make a stock "cheap." So, what we're trying to do is number one, find them when they are cheap and more importantly, see if there is a reason they can get back into the good graces of investors and perhaps become a growth stock or a stock that's attractive to growth investors.

What we've found over a really long period of time is that if you catch that change, where they go from this very cheap valued stock, to one where they become one with promising growth, you're going to capture most of that stock's performance, and that's what we mean when we talk about that. As far as our themes go, we break our long investments up into things like assets placed, turnarounds, undervalued growth stories, and broken IPOs, but that's sort of an after-the-fact look as to what we're doing. When we're looking at things to invest in, that first part of what we do is about the valuation.

Dave: Are there any specific criteria? That's sort of a broad overview of how you approach investing, but are there specific criteria? Obviously you're going to look at management very closely, but what other things are you looking for? Obviously low PEs, but can you be a little more specific?

Bill: Sure, definitely.

> Actually the first things that we look at are two statistics that as value investors are very, very important: price-to-book and price-to-sales. And we use them for reasons that are very simple. Price-to-book, we want them to buy things that are close to book or even below book if we can. Sometimes you can do that, sometimes you can't, but if you buy things at a very, very low valuation to book, when you're wrong, you don't get beat up too much. But when you're right, you get a multiple of that and you can make a lot of money.

We use the price-to-sales metric because many of the companies that we're looking at, and in fact almost all of them, are underearning when we're looking at them. So what we do is take their sales and we try to apply what would be normalized margins, normalized earnings, and come up with a valuation that the stock could sell at in the future, if they were to turn around their operations.

So those are the two things we use mostly, we tend not to use PE because as I said, most of the companies that we're buying are going through some difficult times and their earnings tend to be understated. So they are either going to have a very high PE, or perhaps no PE at all, if they're not making money.

Dave: You know about a year and a half ago, I brought you MusclePharm, a company that Phil Frost invested in. I think it went from $6 to about $14 dollars.

Bill: Right.

Dave: I don't think you invested in that one, but I wanted to bring that up because every now and again I do have a winner (chuckle).

Bill: (Laugh) Well you know we can't find all the great ones.

Dave: Right. You're heavy, 30% of the opportunity fund is in Information Technology and then Industrials and Energy. Well let's go with Information Technology. Why so heavily weighted in that sector?

Bill: Sure, traditionally it's been an area that we spend a lot of time and have a lot of investments in. Principally because of the nature of that business. Most of the small tech companies tend to have a lot of cash, so when difficulties find themselves onto their balance sheet or their income statements, they have the money to get through it. So if they missed a product cycle, or if sales were really bad, or they need to invest more, they're in a great position to do that so they can live out that difficult time by investing the cash that they have and survive for that time when the sun shines for them, if you will. So those things tend to be very good, plus when they're out of favor when people don't like tech stocks they tend to sell at very, very low multiples, and they'll sell as low as the cash on the balance sheet. Conversely, when things are going well for them, growth investors tend to give them very, very big multiples. So for a fund like ours where we like the turnaround stories and we like to buy things at very, very low valuations, they fit perfectly.

A lot of our tech is, they call it *tech*, but it's really a lot of capital goods. So much of what is technology in the market today isn't really high tech. It's not the latest thing, it's not a gadget, it's not a mobile device, but it's really part of the capital goods cycle. So you could say that some of those things that we list as technology are really industrial as well.

Dave: And you seem to like Energy stocks.

Bill: What we do in Energy is mostly with the service industries. We don't feel like we're qualified to pick which stocks will have the best E&P book or best results, but we do know in a world where so many have been successful in North America, that the services provided to those wells, to those E&P companies, are going to get used.

They're nice businesses, they generate a tremendous amount of cash when they're busy, as they have been, with all the shale work in North America, and that's what those investments reflected. We have trimmed them back a little bit, but now with this recent pullback in the market, they are actually starting to look very attractive again.

Dave: Why is there a pullback now on the cyclical stocks, what's happening?

Bill: Well, the beginning of the year everyone was scared the rates were going to go up, so there was a rush out the exits for small caps because there is a perception that they weren't going to get financing as easily as they needed to be, which is interesting because since '08, so many of our companies are in much better shape than they were as far as balance sheets go, so a lot of them don't need to borrow money as much as they used to.

Recently, it's been growth that is scary, part of the equation here, most of the growth concerns have been overseas and most of the growth issues in the United States have been onto the upside, not to the downside. Nonetheless, there has been, over the last two years, a big gap between the performance of big and small-caps and it's purely coincidental. I mean it makes no difference whether you are big or small, the market doesn't really care about that, they care about your earnings.

> I don't know what the chief worry is now, but our worry always with small-caps, especially a fund that focuses on turnarounds and growth, is we want to make sure that they will still have some nice wind in your back. When you have small-caps that are relying on management to turn around a tough situation, it's much easier for them to do that when you have an economic wind in your back versus one in your face.

Dave: What's your top pick, market cap under $500 million?

Bill: I can't give you specific names, since we've been so busy buying and selling that if I give you something and we turn around and have to sell a little of it, I'm gonna have compliance issues, but I will tell you this: The market has pulled back so significantly, so strongly, that many of the names we own are the ones we are adding to, so we continue to take these themes that have worked for us in nonresidential construction, some of the consumer names we think are terrific, especially when you consider what has happened to the cost of energy and what will happen to the cost of food going forward. If you pull out a commodities page and see that most things, I think with the exception of coffee, are down double-digits and most of those things that are down double-digits are down 20-plus percent, the consumer should be in pretty good shape as the year goes on.

We've got very, very easy comps coming from last Christmas, last winter was awful. Christmas was on a Wednesday last year, which was also not a good thing, so we like consumer names as well, so a lot of the retailers, a lot of the teen-based retailers, a lot of the mall-based retailers we think offer pretty good value, once you have a pretty good fourth quarter as well.

Dave: The economies of Europe, China, we have slower growth. How does that affect your decision making in buying smaller-cap stocks?

Bill: I mean you have to be aware of these things. The latest thing to worry about is Germany. Some of the data has been very, very poor. In our fund, a vast majority of the names are U.S. companies; we do have some that are based overseas for headquarters, things like shipping companies, but it's a fund that focuses on the economy in North America. But whether it's an Industrial or Tech, we do have exposure overseas, and many of the markets, whether they be steel or other metals, are affected by world prices, so you have to keep in touch with what's happening. It isn't the most important thing, but on the margin it's going to be the difference between some companies making their earnings or not.

So it's there, you look at it, and we're a stock-by-stock selection type of fund, but we don't ignore the big picture, and there are concerns about growth and it's coming at a time when the United States looks like it's really coming out of those growth concerns, so it's difficult to figure out where this is going to end up, whether the United States will pick up the rest of the world or whether the rest of the world will drop the United States into their problems, but we'll see.

Dave: Bill, in your stock picking career, what's your worst pick ever? The worst mistake you've made?

Bill: Worst mistake? I won't give you one specific name, but I will tell you typically what happens in a fund. Often in a fund like this, and when you are buying things that are cheap, you will find a company that is going through a difficult product cycle, so they'll have a new product or new types of products that are going to be released shortly, and their old products, which are either out of date or no one wants anymore, are falling off and sometimes you'll get caught more than once, probably in my case, where the new product gets delayed and the old product sort of falls off a lot faster than you thought, so you have this gap in revenues, gap in earnings and you get a further pullback from what you thought were already cheap prices based on expectations on earnings. You tend to get that a lot, it comes with the territory.

Dave: What words of wisdom would you share with small-cap investors who are trying to pick these stocks on their own?

Bill: The thing that we do that I think works best for this type of fund and these types of stocks is to buy them over time.

> We don't try to pick the bottom, we don't try to say this is as cheap as it's going to get, because you learn, especially in markets like we have now, that no price is too low, right?

If you think something is so cheap because its $5 and it's got $4 in cash and it's generating good earnings, you say it can't go below that and you come in tomorrow and you see it's $4.50. Then it's $4.25, when you're in a bad market like we are in right now, liquidity dries up and people just want to get out. They want to get names off their portfolios, they don't want to look at them anymore, they don't want them on their screens, and they'll just sell them so they become numbers, they don't represent any value; they don't represent any earnings potential or what the business could ultimately sell at. It's just becomes a number, so trying to pick a specific spot to buy a stock is very, very difficult.

So the best thing that we do, I think, is we buy them over time, getting as best an average price as we can because unfortunately no one is waiting there to sell you everything at the bottom because the sellers are pretty smart, too, so our best defense against that is to buy very smart, too. To buy things slowly over time, to get them at the best average price you can.

Dave: And you've done pretty well. Five-year track record, I think, on the Opportunity Fund is somewhere around 15%, correct? And three years is 23%, so you have done quite well (actual annual average total return for five years is 23.48% and 15.43% for three years). In closing, we talked about Information Technology, Industrials; are there any particular sectors we should be focused on right now, given this pullback? You mentioned a few earlier, but maybe reiterate for us in a closing statement.

Bill: Sure, what we read, what we see, what we hear from our companies, the nonresidential construction market in North America is very good, so whether you're making structural steel carpet tiles, architectural steel, architectural glass, all those parts of the nonresidential construction seem to be gaining momentum. It seems to be across the country, so six months and nine months ago you had certain areas of the country like Texas doing better, but now that seems to be spreading to the secondary markets, the tertiary markets, and usually these are things that last a while, so they don't just stop on a dime, if the market sort of looks soft, usually it's going to carry through the market.

Royce Opportunity Funds Top 10 Positions

Royce Opportunity Fund: Top 10 Positions

Company	% of Net Assets (Subject to Change)
Microsemi Corporation	0.9%
Commercial Metals	0.9
General Cable	0.9
Advanced Energy Industries	0.9
Interface	0.8
Encore Wire	0.8
Mueller Industries	0.8
Astec Industries	0.8
TRC Companies	0.8
Invacare Corporation	0.8

Source: Thomson Reuters Corporation

Royce Micro-Cap Opportunity Fund: Top 10 Positions

Company	% of Net Assets (Subject to Change)
General Cable	2.7%
Applied Optoelectronics	2.5
Power Solutions International	2.4
U.S. Concrete	2.4
Exar Corporation	2.3
EarthLink Holdings	2.3
Trinity Biotech ADR Cl. A	2.2
Zumiez	2.1
Carbonite	2.0
Installed Building Products	2.0

Source: Thomson Reuters Corporation

CHAPTER 4

Dr. Phil Frost

For me, the fun is to build, not to manage. I look for what's available, what is possible to do. That's the overriding consideration. There are a lot of things I would have liked to do, but didn't have the means.

—Dr. Phil Frost, Chairman, OPKO Health

Occupation: Chairman, OPKO Health, Inc.

Age: 78

Education: BA in French Literature, University of Pennsylvania; MD, Albert Einstein College of Medicine

Estimated Net Worth: $4.4 billion

Status: Married 54 years

Residence: Miami

Nickname: "Doctor Midas"

Forbes #112 Richest Men in America

The son of a Jewish shoemaker in Philadelphia, Dr. Phil Frost is a legend in the world of microcaps, a true Titan of Wall Street. We could say of him what *Rolling Stone* said of Jimi Hendrix: He is number one, the best, and everyone else is second.

Frost is by far the most educated and well-rounded Superstar in microcaps and perhaps in all of Wall Street. He is a modern-day Renaissance man, a doctor by training, fluent in French, a venture capitalist, art collector, investor, educator, philanthropist, and inventor. He is also one of the wealthiest men in the world, ranked #112 on the Forbes 400 richest men in America in 2015. Like John Pappajohn, whom you will meet later in the book, Frost developed a strong work ethic early in life. At age 13, he began working in a hardware store after school and on weekends.

At age 15, Frost enrolled in Central High in Philadelphia, one of the top-rated high schools in the country. After graduating from Central High, he attended the University of Pennsylvania, where he studied French Literature, earning a B.A. in 1957. He then received a full scholarship from the Albert Einstein College of Medicine, where he earned an MD specializing in dermatology. While earning his MD, he worked at the National Institutes of Health.

At the age of 32, while still a professor of dermatology at the University of Miami, he invented a medical device used for skin biopsies and within two years sold it for a small profit. The selling of that device led to a career focused on starting, building, financing, buying, and investing in small companies, with a particular focus on healthcare and biotechnology.

He also served as a Lieutenant Commander of the U.S. Public Health Service at the National Cancer Institute from 1963 to 1965. In 1972, he was named chairman of the Department of Dermatology at Mt. Sinai Medical Center in Miami Beach, Florida. While serving as chairman he also ran his own private medical practice.

In 1972, he and a lawyer who worked for Miles Laboratories, named Michael Jaharis, invested in Key Pharmaceuticals, a fledgling company with revenue of $1.5 million and losses of $700,000. Frost quickly raised $250,000 from a bank in Miami, allowing them to continue as a going concern. Over the next several years, his team solved a major problem with Key's lead product, a cough suppressant. They discovered that when combined with a bronchodilator, the suppressant produced a chemical that if time released treated asthma. The asthma medicine, theophylline, had been around for 50 years, but before Key Pharmaceuticals created a new time-released delivery system, it was ineffective due to unsolved toxicity issues. This product, named Theo-Dur, was then tested by the University of Florida with superb results (the company did not have the funds to test it).

In 1977, the FDA approved the drug. Five years later revenue reached $100 million, with Theo-Dur making up 75% of the sales. The company's strategy was based on taking approved drugs and creating better delivery systems using time-released technology. Their next big hit was a product called Nitro-Dur, a bandage coated with nitroglycerin that treated angina pectoris.

Over the next 10 years, Frost continued to grow the company through a series of acquisitions and strategic partnerships. In 1986 he sold the company to Schering Plough for $800 million. He was 51 years old at the time of the sale. He was now worth $100 million. There are several lessons here for investors. First, leadership is paramount in small companies. If Frost and Jaharis had not invested in and taken control of Key Pharmaceuticals, the story may have turned out far differently than it did. Second, he used partnerships with bigger companies to access capital and deepen the research capabilities of the company. Third, he put some very smart people around him, including his first partner, Michael Jaharis, who had 18 years of experience in big pharma. Fourth, he invested in a company that was in a space he knew something about. He stayed within his area of expertise.

An article published by *Miami Herald* writer John Dorschner, in January 2013, quotes an investment banker named Bill Allen, who has known Frost for more than 40 years. Allen said of Frost, "He's not afraid to take risks. He knows the intimate details of the chemistry of products, and he's the kind of guy who can examine 50 deals while eating a sandwich."[1] I was in Dr. Frost's office with RedChip client Drone Aviation (OTCQB: DRNE) when he made the decision to invest $1 million in the company. His questions were incisive and to the point. He cut to the key issues quickly. The meeting lasted only about 15 minutes.

Frost, quoted in Dorschner's article, summed up his philosophy and one of his keys to success:

> *For me, the fun is to build, not to manage. I look for what's available, what is possible to do. That's the overriding consideration. There are a lot of things I would have liked to do, but didn't have the means.*[2]

After his success with Key Pharmaceuticals, his next major venture would test his capacity for overcoming adversity and require years of disciplined effort to make it successful, but would ultimately make him one of the richest men in America.

In 1987, he founded a public chemicals company and merged three other companies into it with the idea of developing new drugs. However, he found it difficult and expensive to develop and get new drugs to market, so he changed the strategy of the company to focus on generic drugs, renaming the company IVAX. He realized that there was an opportunity to establish a niche, producing and selling generic drugs in the United States, Europe, and Latin America. New regulations in the United States had made it easier to sell off patent drugs. Moreover, it was a much less expensive value proposition than investing hundreds of millions in developing new drugs that could take 10 to 15 years to get to market.

> Frost essentially pioneered the launch of generic drugs in Europe and
> Latin America where there was little competition. Remarkably, in just
> seven years, he grew the company to almost $1 billion in sales and $81
> million in net income.

Through strategic acquisitions, partnerships with big pharma, and by
building a world-class R&D team, Frost created one of the world's largest
producers of generic drugs.

However, in the late 1990s, competition for generic drugs intensified,
sales at IVAX declined, and the company began losing money, so Frost and
his team refocused their R&D efforts. In 2001, they launched the Easi-Breathe®
inhaler, a delivery system for albuterol, a time-released medicine that prevents
asthma attacks. This product was a major factor in making the company profitable again.

In 2005, a large Israeli company, the world's largest maker of generic
drugs, Teva Pharmaceutical Industries (NYSE: TEVA; shown in Figure 4.1),
purchased IVAX for $7.4 billion. Frost made $1.1 billion on this transaction.
He was now 68 years old.

As he was building IVAX, he also invested in dozens of other companies in a variety of industries, including banks, high-tech, metals and mining, consumer goods, and his specialty, healthcare companies. Frost is still
active in the capital markets. He is considered by many the high priest of
the microcap world and is admired and respected by entrepreneurs, bankers, brokers, fund managers, scientists, and doctors worldwide.

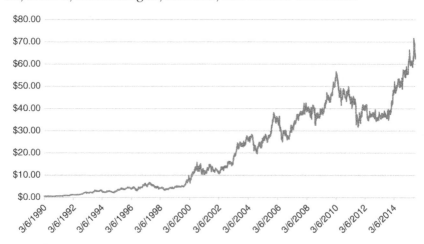

FIGURE 4.1 Teva Pharmaceutical Industries Limited (NYSE: TEVA)
Data Source: Thomson Reuters Corporation.

He is now in the process of building what I believe will become the masterpiece of his career: OPKO Health (NYSE: OPK), a vertically integrated company that Frost likens to a mini-Berkshire Hathaway of the healthcare industry. In an interview with Phil Frost for my show, he shared his vision for OPKO Health, which has a market cap of $5.78 billion (as of September 8, 2015). I will note also that Frost, the chairman of OPKO, has purchased nearly $31 million of OPKO stock over the past 24 months.

OPKO Health (Figure 4.2) is a pharmaceutical and diagnostics company with a wide range of products and drugs under development and four potential blockbuster technologies addressing a combined $10 billion market.

One of its lead products is a treatment for chronic liver disease, which is in a phase III clinical trial. They are also working on a biomarker for Alzheimer's. Also under development is "a protein-based influenza vaccine that would offer protection against influenza." In clinical development are also various therapeutic agents for respiratory disorders, including products for asthma, chronic obstructive pulmonary disease, and chronic cough.[3]

I asked him why he has invested so much of his time and money in OPKO Health. His answer:

> *I like to invest in situations that give me an opportunity for a very big return. By that I mean that over a reasonable period of time, I can leverage the investment to realize significant returns above and beyond what's available in the money markets and such funds.*

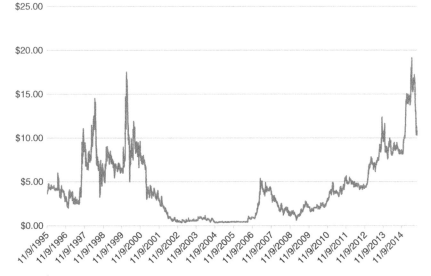

FIGURE 4.2 OPKO Health, Inc. (NYSE: OPKO)
Data Source: Thomson Reuters Corporation.

One of my final questions in the interview: "What is the process you undertake to determine whether to invest in a technology or company? What are you looking for?"

"We look for potential for big products with big returns. But also we like to have products that may fit with other products that we are developing, that are in the same field as the other products that we are working on so that we're not totally a game of isolated products. And as time goes on, we'll have areas of [particular focus] of course, but right now we're very open and still in an exploring phase and inquisitive of anything that seems to be reasonable with respect to price and big with respect to profits."

OPKO also invests in dozens of other healthcare companies, including several past and current RedChip client companies, including Sorrento Therapeutics (NASDAQ: SRNE), which he sold in December 2013 for a 1,000% return (Figure 4.3), Sevion Therapeutics (OTCQB: SNTI), and Ruthigan (NASDAQ: RTGN).

We have a very unusual model, because in addition to what we've talked about, we also have investments in a significant number of other companies that have breakthrough technologies, and we look at these as opportunities to make money from appreciation in their value, but at the same time we like to have access to some of the products that might come from these companies.

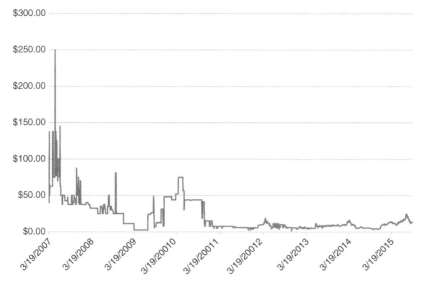

FIGURE 4.3 Sorrento Therapeutics (NASDAQ: SRNE)
Data Source: Thomson Reuters Corporation.

Frost also invests personally in a cornucopia of microcap stocks, including IZEA (OTCQB: IZEA), Drone Aviation (OTCQB: DRNE), ChromaDex (OTCQB: CDXC), and MusclePharm (OTCQB: MSLP), all present or past RedChip clients.

He is chairman of Ladenburg Thalmann (NYSE: LTS), a public Miami-based investment bank focused primarily on small-caps. The stock has appreciated 118% over the past 12 months and earnings are up 100%. The Street.com recently put a "Buy" rating on the stock.

There are several important lessons that emerge from the Phil Frost story. First, investors would be wise to follow his investments and perhaps invest, if possible, when he does. Keep in mind, however, that most of his investments are in private transactions, meaning he buys stock directly from the company, many times at a substantial discount to market prices. Second, investors should understand that what may appear to be a losing situation on the surface may hold great promise for the future.

One product, one technology, can turn a company around with the right management team. Remember Key Pharmaceuticals' lead product, a cough suppressant, appeared to be unmarketable until Frost and his research team figured out that with a time-released delivery system using a bronchodilator, it treated asthma with amazing results.

> One man, one woman, can change the direction and dynamics of a company. Look closely at who sits on the board of directors, the advisory board, and of course, upper management. Look for companies who are spending heavily on research and development. Finally, invest in what you know, in areas you understand. Frost did not go outside his area of expertise early in his career.

Business Advice from Dr. Phil Frost

1. Education is important. Frost is a highly educated man. His knowledge in science and medicine has been very helpful in his analysis and evaluation of companies and products in the healthcare space. Remember, in addition to his degree in French Literature, he also has an MD.

2. He puts highly capable people around him, such as Steve Rubin, Michael Jaharis, Bill Allen, Mike Weintraub, and Michael Brauser.

3. He relentlessly pursues his mission in the face of adversity but is willing to change directions if things are not working. Remember IVAX. He changed the strategy from developing new drugs to marketing generic drugs where there was little competition.

4. He did not invest heavily in companies outside his areas of expertise, but did what he could do at the moment with the resources he
had.

Dr. Frost, like John Pappajohn, has been a major benefactor of the
arts and education. He has donated hundreds of millions to philanthropic
causes. In 2003, he donated $33 million to the School of Music at the Uni-
versity of Miami. In 2011, he donated $35 million toward the construction of
the new Miami Science Museum building at Bicentennial Park in Downtown
Miami. He serves on the Board of Regents of the Smithsonian Institution,
and is a Trustee of the Scripps Research Institute.

Phillip Frost Top Stock Positions

Frost Phillip, MD, et al.

Company	Ticker	Position (m)	Value ($m)
Ladenburg Thalmann Financial Services Inc.	NYSE: LTS	55.57	187.28
ChromaDex Corp.	OTC: CDXC	15.25	18.15
Non-Invasive Monitoring Systems Inc.	OTC: NIMU	15.00	2.55

Source: Thomson Reuters Corporation.

Frost Gamma Investments Trust

Company	Ticker	Position (m)	Value ($m)
OPKO Health Inc.	NYSE: OPK	154.97	1676.72
Cocrystal Pharma Inc.	OTC: COCP	103.56	123.75
Neovasac Inc.	NASDAQ: NVC	14.79	100.24
Pershing Gold Corp.	NASDAQ: PGLC	3.04	13.20
American DG Energy Inc.	NYSE: ADGE	2.63	6.44
Cadiz Inc.	NASDAQ: CDZI	0.80	5.56
Cocrystal Pharma Inc.	OTC: COCP	12.34	4.75
MusclePharm Corp.	OTC: MSLP	0.67	4.75
Sevion Therapeutics Inc.	OTC: SVON	1.56	4.38
Wright Investors Service Holdings Inc.	OTC: WISH	1.32	2.65
USell.com Inc.	OTC: USEL	0.60	1.70
Prism Technologies Group, Inc.	NASDAQ: PTNT	0.50	1.67

Company	Ticker	Position (m)	Value ($m)
MV Portfolios Inc.	OTC: MVPI	0.92	1.57
Arno Therapeutics Inc.	OTC: ARNI	0.69	1.53
Vaporin Inc.	OTC: VAPO	0.41	1.34
Alliqua Inc.	NASDAQ: ALQA	0.26	0.96
Great West Resources Inc.	OTC: GWST	0.13	0.86

Source: Thomson Reuters Corporation.

Notes

1. John Dorschner, "Billionaire Phil Frost an 'Entrepreneur's Entrepreneur,'" *Miami Herald*, January 6, 2013.
2. Ibid.
3. Reuters, "Profile: OPKO Health Inc. (OPK)," www.reuters.com/finance/stocks/companyProfile?symbol=OPK.

CHAPTER 5

Dave Maley

Invest in something you can get your arms around and be very conservative, own enough stock so that you are not putting all your eggs in one basket.

—Dave Maley, Fund Manager, Ariel Discovery Fund

Occupation: Fund Manager, Ariel Discovery Fund

Money Under Management: $600 million

Age: 53

Education: BSc in Business, Notre Dame; MBA, University of Chicago

Status: Married, two children

Residence: Chicago, IL

First Job on Wall Street: Goldman Sachs

Favorite Book: *Margin of Safety*, Seth Klarman

Favorite Stock: RealNetworks Inc. (NASDAQ: RNWK)

Hobbies: Reading financial books and spy novels; running marathons

David Maley went to college thinking he would be a doctor or an engineer, but then he took a class called "Investments," and then another, "Advanced Investments," both taught by Sarkis Joseph Khoury, PhD, a prominent economist, academic, and consultant specializing in international finance, debt restructuring, and speculative markets. Taking these classes changed Maley's thinking about what he wanted to do with his life. In 1981, while in his junior year at the University of Notre Dame, he changed his major to Business. Two years later he graduated in the top 5% of his class. He then earned his MBA at the University of Chicago Booth School of Business.

In 1984, Dave Maley launched his Wall Street career as an institutional sales representative at the premiere investment bank in the world, Goldman Sachs. He spent eight years at Goldman Sachs calling on large institutions, pitching blue-chip stocks and derivative products. "I was on the wrong side at Goldman. I like picking stocks. The more you focus on smaller-caps, the more you can make a difference. They require more research, more study, but with it comes the opportunity to outperform the market," he explains. After leaving Goldman Sachs in 1992, he worked for the Harris Trust fund as a portfolio manager, focusing on large-cap stocks, managing money for wealthy families. It was there that he began to develop an interest in small-cap stocks.

In the process, he got to know John Rogers, who founded Ariel Investments in the 1980s. In 2002, he launched his own long-only, small cap value fund with $2 million of capital. His performance was good enough to earn the attention of John Rogers, who placed several million dollars of Ariel's corporate cash with his fund.

His performance over the next seven years would lead Rogers to offer Maley a job in 2009. Maley moved his existing microcap strategy to Ariel Investments, where within three years it grew from under $10 million to more than $600 million. In 2011, he launched Ariel Small-Cap Discovery Fund to complement the microcap separate account strategy.

He characterizes the fund in this way: "We have created a strategy that gives excess returns in a low risk way. We are not a wild, gun slinging portfolio. We have a much lower volatility than many microcap funds. Our standard deviation is closer to the S&P 500."

He explains that "the institutional neglect of sell-side coverage from most of the large money management firms who simply don't care about microcaps allows us to find opportunities that are relatively undiscovered. The stocks we find are special situations, they are idiosyncratic, you might say."

He is sector agnostic. He has invested in retailers, waste disposable companies, toy companies, and aerospace. "It runs the gamut," he says. "We look for mispricing based on a set of strict criteria. We always look for a margin of safety, for some deep value, which is usually based on assets."

Maley's thinking about the market was influenced by two professors from the University of Chicago Booth School of Business, Lars Peter Hansen and Eugene Fama, both of whom won the Nobel Memorial Prize in Economic Sciences in 2013. Fama, who received his PhD from the University of Chicago, was a professor at the Booth School while Maley was earning his MBA. In fact, Maley's first finance class was taught by Dr. Fama, who is considered the father of the efficient market hypothesis.

As for Dr. Lars Hansen, his major contributions to the understanding of financial markets is his "theory of generalized method of moments," which he developed in 1982 (the year Maley started his MBA program). His theory is "widely applied in finance for studying market efficiency and understanding models for asset markets."[1]

It is worth considering their work in light of the long-running debate on whether stocks are efficient and rational. Do their prices reflect their true value, responding to all available information about the company, or are they unpredictable and often inefficient, meaning they take too long to reflect all the information that is available about the company?

Both Hansen's and Fama's research provides empirical evidence using statistical models that while we cannot predict the future short-term prices of assets, including stocks, we can predict long-term prices with a high degree of accuracy. In other words, stocks behave rationally in the longer term.

This debate is particularly relevant as it relates to microcaps, as by their very nature they are the most volatile asset class and include less developed companies with shorter track records; moreover, the entire basis for buying microcap companies is the belief that they are significantly undervalued and they are not behaving rationally at the time one buys them, but will at some point in the future, potentially offering the opportunity for a high return on investment.

To digress again for a moment to better illustrate the point, when Quadrant 4 Systems (OTCQB: QFOR) was trading at $0.06 with a $5 million market cap in July 2013, was it trading efficiently? On August 23, 2013, the stock traded 484,800 shares, closing at $0.17, up from $0.11 from the day before. The next day the stock doubled again on 656,400 shares, closing at $0.35 (Figure 5.1). In just 48 hours, the Street said the company was worth $30 million or 3× more than it was two days before.

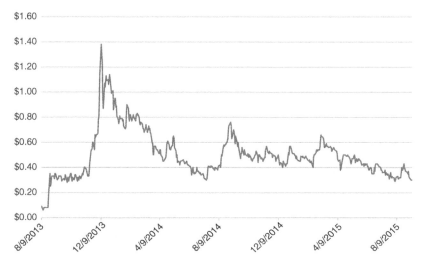

FIGURE 5.1 Quadrant 4 Systems (OTCQB: QFOR)
Data Source: Thomson Reuters Corporation.

On November 13, 2013, Quadrant 4 announced record third-quarter revenue and EBITDA and record nine-month revenue of $28 million, up 41% over the same period in the previous year. The stock on November 12 was $0.33. Over the next four weeks, November 13, 2013, through December 13, 2013, the stock would continue to appreciate, reaching $0.93 on December 5. On December 6, Quadrant 4 issued a press release that, for the first time, clearly explained their healthcare exchange platform and the market opportunity for the technology behind it. That day, the stock traded 1,287,000 shares and closed at $1.14. The next day it traded 1,036,800 shares, closing at an all-time-high of $1.38, now with a market cap of $105 million. The carefully written press release was, in form if not essence, new information to the Street. It appeared that the stock was becoming efficient.

Some investors, having bought the stock at between $0.06 and $0.20, were now up 700%. Some were up almost 2,000%. The stock naturally did not hold the high, but did hold over 50% of the gain. But is it today fairly valued? Is the stock efficient given all the information that is publicly available about the company? The point is, each individual investor will decide, be it a hedge fund, institution, accredited investor, or retail broker, whether it is fairly valued today.

The highlights of the press release announcing the 2013 Nobel Prize Winners in Economic Sciences "for their empirical analysis of asset prices" sheds some light on the efficient market debate.

> *There is no way to predict the price of stocks and bonds over the next few days or weeks. But it is quite possible to foresee the broad course of these prices over longer periods, such as the next three to five years. These findings, which might seem both surprising and contradictory, were made and analyzed by this year's Laureates. . . .*
>
> *Beginning in the 1960s, Eugene Fama and several collaborators demonstrated that stock prices are extremely difficult to predict in the short run, and that new information is very quickly incorporated into prices. . . .*
>
> *If prices are nearly impossible to predict over days or weeks, then shouldn't they be even harder to predict over several years? The answer is no, as Robert Shiller discovered in the early 1980s.*[2]

The efficient market hypothesis has been challenged by academics and financial experts for decades. Benoit Mandelbrot, in his book, *The Misbehavior of Markets*, referring to the work of Alan J. Marcus, a Boston college finance professor, notes that Peter Lynch's Magellan Fund "beat the market by an average 25% a year." He also notes that "the odds of that occurring by dumb luck are less than one in 10,000—'far beyond the bounds of luck in an efficient market,' concluded the study's author, Alan J. Marcus. . . ."[3]

For example, we read in Alan J. Marcus' description of his class, Workshop in Behavioral Finance, that: "Extensive psychological research has documented that people tend to be overconfident in their judgments. People tend to show a wishful thinking bias, believing what they want to believe."

It is also worth considering the work of Robert J. Shiller, Sterling Professor of Economics at Yale University, also a recipient of the 2013 Nobel Prize in Economic Sciences (cocreator of the Case–Shiller housing price index). He argues that there are always psychological and behavioral issues at play in the markets and they often create inefficiencies in the market.

The study of behavior indicates that "people show problems of self-control. . . . People tend to exhibit belief perseverance, hanging onto past beliefs long after they should have abandoned them. People tend to make the error of anchoring, that is, when making difficult quantitative judgments they tend to start from some arbitrary initial estimate, often suggested to them by something in their immediate environment, and evidence that comes easily to mind, thereby allowing their decisions to be overinfluenced by evidence that is more salient and attention-grabbing" (see Robert J. Shiller's book, *Irrational Exuberance*).[4] Sometimes microcaps reach market capitalizations that are clearly irrational relative to their fundamentals and peer-group multiples.

> The stock market is not simply a digital machine executing trades, reflecting buy and sell orders, and recording price movements. The market does not operate as an island unto itself. The market is an extension of the investors who bring it to life every day, investors who breathe into it all their prejudices, presuppositions, knowledge and lack of knowledge, needs, hopes, and fears, both rational and irrational. Apply this truth to the microcap asset class and we are left with volatility and inefficiencies extraordinaire.

A good example of Shiller's hypothesis at work is the irrational and unpredictable lightning-fast run-up of marijuana stocks in 2013. One stock in particular is worthy of mention to help illustrate our point. Medbox (OTCQB: MDBX), until recently a nonreporting pink-sheet stock that went public via a reverse merger in August 2012 at $2.00, sells marijuana dispensing machines and a vaporizer technology for smoking marijuana.

The stock surged to $200 a few weeks after going public, reaching a market cap of over $1 billion. Though it touched $100 only for a moment,

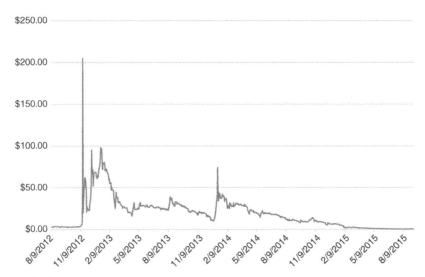

FIGURE 5.2 Medbox (PNK: MDBX)
Data Source: Thomson Reuters Corporation.

it continued to trade in the $40 range for months, then eventually drifted down to $5 per share, then shot up again to $45.00 in a week-long run in January 2014 after the CEO appeared on CNBC. October 9, 2014, it sported a $275 million market cap (Figure 5.2).

The company reported $728,000 in revenue for the first six months of 2014 with a $2.7 million loss. Is it trading efficiently? Investors believe what they want to believe, and they do not all think alike.

Maley's Core Investment Principles in His Own Words
1. "We invest at a price so cheap relative to intrinsic value that even if we are wrong about what happens to the companies, we can still do well."
2. "We focus on stocks with $500 million and under market caps; our average market cap is $200 million. We see a lot of mispricing of stocks with market caps under $200 million."
3. "We rarely buy above two times book value, as we like to buy stocks that are trading below tangible value."
4. "We buy below asset value, below liquidation value."
5. "We look for a management team with a good plan."

6. "Our valuation is based sometimes on cash flow, sometimes on a sum of the parts."
7. "We are agnostic; we go where we can find value."
8. "We are very debt adverse; debt should be less than 10% of cash or no more than 20% to 30% of market cap."
9. "With cash, a company can survive tough times, a bad economic environment. Cash provides an anchor to valuation."
10. "If you are buying cheap assets, investors can get hurt if management burns cash too fast, is growing too fast, or does a dumb acquisition."
11. "One of the first things we do when we identify a stock that looks interesting is study the proxy statement and look at insider ownership and corporate governance."
12. "We don't want management to get rich if shareholders can't do well."
13. "We like a lot of insider ownership, bonuses tied to performance, board members who own a lot of stock, and an outside chairman who has skin in the game is important to us."
14. "We are very long-term investors—we don't talk about quarter-to-quarter revenue and earnings. We talk about long-long-term investing. Our average holding period is three to five years."
15. "We will buy companies that are not profitable if there is a discount to asset value."
16. "We must get a sense of cash flow, asset burn, cash burn."
17. "We ask, 'How much of a discount are we buying?'"

Market Leader (NASDAQ: LEDR) is representative of the type of company in which Maley invests. A software company for the residential real estate market, Market Leader sells a subscription-based real estate marketing software and runs national real estate websites. In the third quarter of 2013, Trulia (NYSE: TRLA), a powerhouse that is sparring with Zillow for dominance of the real estate software and listing market, purchased Market Leader for $11.33 per share (Figures 5.3 and 5.4). Maley initially began buying the stock in 2010 at 1.68 when a 200,000-share block became available.

Though Market Leader was losing money in 2010, when he began positioning in the stock, Maley liked the fact that they had $2.25 per share in cash, and zero debt. "I saw a great idea and a strong management team capable of executing and an innovative product the real estate industry wanted and needed." In 2010, the company was transitioning to a SaaS (software-as-a-service) model, which Maley knew would dramatically improve margins. In 2011, the company announced a deal to be on every desk of every Keller Williams representative in the country, a 100,000-unit order. "This was no longer a pure asset situation," he says.

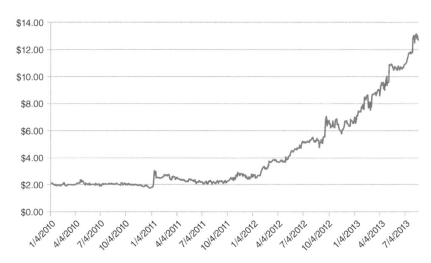

FIGURE 5.3 Market Leader (NASDAQ: LEDR)
Data Source: Thomson Reuters Corporation.

FIGURE 5.4 Trulia, Inc. (NYSE: TRLA)
Data Source: Thomson Reuters Corporation.

No financial model has ever been developed that guarantees success all the time, every time. When I asked Maley about his worst stock pick, he paused for a moment, sighed, and lamented:

> *"I bought an E&P company that leased small properties and did an excellent job of exploiting them. They kept a clean balance sheet.*

> *The company was doing well for years. But then the CEO decided he wanted to make an acquisition that would double the size of the company, so he levered up, acquired the target. Within two years, they went bankrupt.*

"My mistake was staying with a company who levered up to transform the company. The balance sheet went to hell. Now I ask the CEOs of the companies I am considering buying, 'Is there any worry I wake up one day and you have $50 million in debt because you made an acquisition?'"

Maley says, "We never try to game a stock, buy on the basis of what is going on in the short term. We create a good two-way dialogue with management making sure that we clearly understand how they approach capital allocation. We bring two or three members of our team to meet with management. We will challenge their thinking, play devil's advocate to test their thesis."

Maley has been influenced by the thinking of Seth Klarman, a billionaire and founder of the Baupost Group, a $25 billion private investment partnership. He is the author of Maley's favorite financial book, *Margin of Safety: Risk-Averse Value Investing Strategies for the Thoughtful Investor.*[5] While not a microcap investor, Baupost's basic investment approach is to buy companies that are out of favor, that may be having problems, but fixable problems. He wants companies that will give him a margin of safety, whose intrinsic value offers a backstop if the company does not execute as he believes they will. For 30 years he has averaged 20% annual returns.[6]

Maley's Favorite Stock: RealNetworks, Inc. (RNWK)

Based in Seattle, RealNetworks is best known for its RealPlayer media player software, which is downloaded onto millions of computers. The company invented the streaming media category in 1995 with the introduction of RealAudio.

The most important part of the company's businesses is the RealPlayer Group. As sales of the legacy products have diminished, the company has developed RealPlayer Cloud, a cloud-centric and mobile-centric video storage and sharing platform. The service has grown from 500,000 to over 10 million users in a year and is approaching levels where Maley believes it will become a meaningful source of value for RealNetworks.

With a current market capitalization of under $185 million, and more than $130 million in cash with no debt, the market is currently ascribing very little value to the company's business (based on a June 30, 2015, share price of $5.41). Even assuming significant cash burn in the near future, and applying a modest multiple to revenues—which should return to growth later this year—Maley comes up with a valuation roughly 40% above current levels.

However, this valuation completely ignores an overlooked and potentially extremely valuable asset. Hidden in plain sight is RealNetworks' 43% stake in privately held Rhapsody, the pioneer of the music streaming business. RealNetworks has made it clear that this is an investment it intends to monetize. Carried on the books at just $7 million, Maley believes the 43% holding is worth at least $5.00 per share and could be worth multiples of that.

Through Napster, Rhapsody's international brand, music is now available in more than 30 countries, up from only 3 just two years ago. A global partnership with Telefonica is showing significant growth, and the company has also expanded into auto partnerships. Finally, Rhapsody and Twitter (TWTR) announced a partnership just weeks ago, giving Rhapsody access to a massive user base.

Reports are that Spotify is earning a value of $500–$600 per subscriber. At the high end, Rhapsody's 3 million subscribers would lead to a valuation of nearly $775 million, or more than $21.00 per share for RealNetworks' 43% share. While Maley uses a heavily discounted version of that calculation to be conservative, he arrives at a sum-of-the parts valuation for RealNetworks of nearly more than 2.5 times the current share prices.

FIGURE 5.5 RealNetworks Inc. (NASDAQ: RNWK)
Data Source: Thomson Reuters Corporation.

Dave Maley's Advice to Investors in His Own Words
- "Invest in something you can get your arms around and be very conservative, own enough stock so that you are not putting all eggs in one basket."
- "If you don't have time to devote to doing your own homework, better to have someone manage your accounts for you."
- "There are a lot of risky companies built on one or two products, be wary of those."
- "Be wary of bad management teams, don't bet on dreams. Do your homework and be careful."

Ariel Top Stock Positions

Ariel Top Stock Positions

		Annualized		
Ariel Micro-Cap Value	**1 Year**	**3 Years**	**5 Years**	**10 Years**
Net of Fees	45.49%	18.64%	24.57%	8.38%

As of March 31, 2015.
Ariel Micro-Cap Value Fund closed.
Source: Thomson Reuters Corporation.

Ariel Small-Cap Value Holdings

Company	Ticker	Position (m)	% Fund Assets
Cash Balance	CASH-1	3.93	7.2
Lazard Ltd.	LAZ	2.59	4.7
Bristow Group Inc.	BRS	2.41	4.4
First American Financial Corp.	FAF	2.4	4.4
JLL	JLL	2.31	4.2
Charles River Laboratories Intl, Inc.	CRL	2.05	3.8
International Speedway Corp.	ISCA	1.99	3.6
Littelfuse, Inc.	LFUS	1.98	3.6
Team, Inc.	TISI	1.9	3.5
MTS Systems Corp.	MTSC	1.75	3.2
Madison Square Garden Co.	MSG	1.74	3.2
Blount Intl, Inc.	BLT	1.74	3.2
TEGNA Inc.	TGNA	1.69	3.1
Zebra Technologies Corp.	ZBRA	1.65	3.0

(Continued)

Company	Ticker	Position (m)	% Fund Assets
Brink's Co.	BCO	1.62	3.0
Kennametal Inc.	KMT	1.6	2.9
Bio-Rad Laboratories, Inc.	BIO	1.6	2.9
Janus Capital Group Inc.	JNS	1.55	2.8
Simpson Manufacturing Co., Inc.	SSD	1.51	2.8
Brady Corp.	BRC	1.39	2.6
Meredith Corp.	MDP	1.37	2.5
U.S. Silica Holdings, Inc.	SLCA	1.21	2.2
Anixter Intl Inc.	AXE	1.2	2.2
Interface, Inc.	TILE	1.13	2.1
Fair Isaac Corp.	FICO	1.1	2.0
IDEX Corp.	IEX	0.88	1.6
PrivateBancorp, Inc.	PVTB	0.86	1.6
Dun & Bradstreet Corp.	DNB	0.83	1.5
Manning & Napier, Inc.	MN	0.72	1.3
Matthews Intl Corp.	MATW	0.71	1.3
Horace Mann Educators Corp.	HMN	0.67	1.2
Middleby Corp.	MIDD	0.61	1.1
Sotheby's	BID	0.58	1.1
HCC Insurance Holdings, Inc.	HCC	0.55	1.0
Rosetta Stone Inc.	RST	0.52	1.0
Lumber Liquidators Holdings, Inc.	LL	0.52	0.9
Bob Evans Farms, Inc.	BOBE	0.47	0.9
Gannett Co Inc.	GCI	0.37	0.7
DeVry Education Group Inc.	DV	0.31	0.6
Contango Oil & Gas Co.	MCF	0.3	0.6
Mitcham Industries, Inc.	MIND	0.28	0.5

Source: Thomson Reuters Corporation.

Ariel Discovery Fund Holdings

Company	Ticker	Position (m)	% Fund Assets
Cowen Group, Inc.	COWN	2.42	6.2
ORBCOMM, Inc.	ORBC	2.24	5.8
Pendrell Corp.	PCO	2.24	5.8
RealNetworks, Inc.	RNWK	1.76	4.6
Capital Southwest Corp.	CSWC	1.71	4.4
Fixed Income Clearing Corporation		1.59	4.1
Century Casinos, Inc.	CNTY	1.53	4.0
Rentech, Inc.	RTK	1.43	3.7
Rosetta Stone Inc.	RST	1.42	3.7

Company	Ticker	Position (m)	% Fund Assets
XO Group Inc.	XOXO	1.33	3.4
Imation Corp.	IMN	1.31	3.4
Furmanite Corp.	FRM	1.30	3.3
PCTEL, Inc.	PCTI	1.25	3.2
First American Financial Corp.	FAF	1.25	3.2
Landec Corp.	LNDC	1.19	3.1
International Speedway Corp.	ISCA	1.13	2.9
Spartan Motors Inc.	SPAR	1.03	2.7
SeaChange Intl, Inc.	SEAC	1.00	2.6
Brooks Automation, Inc.	BRKS	0.95	2.4
Contango Oil & Gas Co.	MCF	0.92	2.4
Gulf Island Fabrication, Inc.	GIFI	0.86	2.2
Team, Inc.	TISI	0.83	2.1
AV Homes, Inc.	AVHI	0.82	2.1
Telenav Inc.	TNAV	0.77	2.0
Superior Industries Intl, Inc.	SUP	0.73	1.9
Rubicon Technology, Inc.	RBCN	0.69	1.8
Orion Energy Systems, Inc.	OESX	0.67	1.7
Erickson Inc.	EAC	0.65	1.7
Kindred Biosciences, Inc.	KIN	0.65	1.7
Simpson Manufacturing Co., Inc.	SSD	0.61	1.6
MB Financial, Inc.	MBFI	0.58	1.5
Brink's Co.	BCO	0.52	1.3
Electro Rent Corp.	ELRC	0.47	1.2
LeapFrog Enterprises, Inc.	LF	0.41	1.1
Mitcham Industries, Inc.	MIND	0.37	0.9
Vical Inc.	VICL	0.31	0.8
Other Assets and Liabilities		−0.19	−0.5

Source: Thomson Reuters Corporation.

Notes

1. Ameet Sachdev and Peter Frost, "Two University of Chicago Professors Win Nobel Prize in Economics," *Chicago Tribune Business,* October 15, 2013.
2. Royal Swedish Academy of Sciences, "Trendspotting in Asset Markets," *The Prize in Economic Sciences 2013,* October 14, 2013.
3. Benoit Mandelbrot and Richard L. Hudson, *The Misbehavior of Markets: A Fractal View of Financial Turbulence* (New York: Basic Books, 2006), p. 103.

4. Robert J. Shiller, *Irrational Exuberance* (Princeton, NJ: Princeton University Press, 2000).
5. Seth A. Klarman, *Margin of Safety: Risk-Averse Value Investing Strategies for the Thoughtful Investor* (New York: HarperCollins, 1991).
6. David Sterman, "How to Invest Like Seth Klarman," *Street Authority*, August 13, 2013.

CHAPTER 6

John Pappajohn

I've made my money by being the first in markets. As a venture capitalist, you have to seek out the cutting-edge companies. You get in as early as possible. That way you make a lot more headway and profits.

—John Pappajohn, Entrepreneur, Philanthropist, Business Leader

Occupation: Venture Capitalist

Age: 87

Education: BSc Business, University of Iowa, Des Moines, 1952

Estimated Net Worth: $600 million

Status: Married 53 years

Residence: Des Moines, Iowa

Advice: "You can't be right all the time, but you can surround yourself with honest people."

Hobbies: Art collector, philanthropist

If you spend time with John Pappajohn, you will notice two things about him right away. One, he shoots his arrows straight; two, though tough as nails, and very wealthy, he carries himself with an air of humility. Born in 1928, an inauspicious year for a man who is today one of the true Titans of Wall Street, at age 85, he is the oldest member of the Microcap Superstar Club. In 2013, *The National Herald*, a prominent publication that chronicles the lives of Greek Americans, ranked him #12 on their annual list of the 50 wealthiest Greeks in America with an estimated net worth of $600 million.[1]

Today he is still very active in the capital markets, spending almost a third of his time in New York meeting with bankers, analysts, fund managers, and CEOs, always on the hunt for new opportunities and looking for ways to help the companies he has financed. He is currently on the board of directors of Cancer Genetics (NASDAQ: CGIX), one of his favorite companies. Founded by a scientist at Memorial Sloan Kettering Cancer Center, who developed DNA-based tests for bloodborne, kidney, and urogenital cancers, he began investing in CGIX when it was still a fledgling private company, struggling to survive with no commercial contracts. Just as the other Superstars in this book have done so many times in their careers, he invested in a struggling company with an innovative technology when others were not willing to take the risk. While still a private company, he provided a badly needed cash infusion. The company is now a NASDAQ-listed company with a rapidly growing institutional following, double-digital revenue growth, six commercial cancer diagnostic tests, a joint venture with the Mayo Clinic, and contracts with major pharmaceutical companies, including Gilead Sciences, Novartis, and Merck.

Led by CEO Panna Sharma, in 2013 the company raised nearly $60 million. The stock reached a 52-week high of $23.25 in the third quarter of 2013, up from $7.00 a few months earlier. John Pappajohn has invested $12 million of his own money in the company. In 2014–2015, the company made two acquisitions, driving revenue for the first six months of 2015 to $8.6, up 191% for the same period in 2014.

> The son of Greek immigrants, whose parents came to Mason City, Iowa, in 1930 when he was only nine months old, he is the epitome of the great American success story. A father who early on taught him the value of hard work, frugality, and integrity nurtured his entrepreneurial spirit.

At the turn of the twentieth century, Mason City was a melting pot of 29 nationalities, with a fast-growing textile-manufacturing sector and a large cement and brick-manufacturing base. Its central location and proximity to water and natural resources made it well suited as a manufacturing hub and it became a major job creator in Iowa and an important contributor to its GDP for several decades. In the 1920s, Greeks were the largest immigrant group in this bustling Midwestern town.

Before he reached the age of 10, his entrepreneurial career began. As a young boy, he collected and sold scrap metal to local businesses to earn spending money. His father, who worked in a textile factory in Mason City, eventually saved enough money to start his own grocery store, where John Pappajohn worked as a butcher after school and on the weekends in high school. When he was 16 years old, John Pappajohn's father died. This was not an easy thing for the son of a first-generation immigrant, particularly in 1943, when America was still recovering from the effects of the Depression and in the midst of World War II. His mother, however, lived for 98 years and was a source of inspiration and encouragement throughout his life, and helped keep him on the straight-and-narrow path. He describes her lovingly as "a good, good woman."

In 1947, he was accepted into the University of Iowa in Des Moines where he majored in Business Administration.

In 1952, after earning his college degree, he took a job selling life insurance. He soon became one of the top producers and moved into upper management. A few years later, while still in his early thirties, he raised $1.5 million from a businessman in Mason City, and started his own life insurance company called The Guardsman. Three years later he took on a partner, appointed him president, and took the company public. According to Pappajohn, his new partner lost focus, mismanaged the enterprise, and the company lost its competitive edge. "The president would sometimes make rash decisions, did not think through the implications of the policies he implemented. I decided it was best if I exited."

Pappajohn sold his stock at $6.00 a share making $100,000, equivalent in today's dollars to about $600,000. He describes that venture as "mildly successful."

> **Lesson one:** Management is critical. Having strong, focused, disciplined leadership at the top is paramount in building a successful company. As an investor in microcaps, one should study the leadership, check their background, and be aware of their past successes and/or failures.

After leaving the insurance business, he and a fraternity brother started a lawnmower manufacturing company. He invested the $100,000 he earned from selling his stock in The Guardsman, secured a loan from his fraternity brother's father for $1.5 million, who happened to own a bank, and began manufacturing lawnmowers. After four years of hard work, he and his partner realized that the profit margins were too small to stay competitive. The company could not compete with companies the size of Hahn, Dayton, and Craftsman, who dominated lawnmower manufacturing in the 1960s and 1970s. They did not have a newer, better technology, nor were they capitalized in a way that would allow them to compete with the sales and marketing efforts of the large manufacturers. After four years of losing money, he decided to exit the business. He did not take this company public. "In retrospect, I was lucky to get my $100,000 back," he said.

> **Lesson two:** Determine whether the company has a technology that is better, different, and more innovative than its competitors. If not, do they have an R&D team, patents, something that will give them an edge in their industry if properly capitalized? Look at a company's profit margins. Are they equal, worse, or better than the industry average? Find out why they are better or worse. What does the company need to change to improve profit margins? Capital? New management? Better technology? Equipment?

John Pappajohn, like Charles Diker and Phil Sassower (Superstars), was one of the pioneers of the venture capital business, which in the 1960s was just coming of age as an organized industry. In 1969, he decided to start his own venture capital fund. He went to a wealthy businessman in Des Moines and asked him to invest. The businessman said he wanted Pappajohn to speak to a professional investor in Nebraska first and that if he gave the okay, he would invest. The man he wanted him to speak to would become one of the wealthiest and most influential people in the world, Warren Buffett.

John Pappajohn, now age 39, still not having made his first million, called the Wizard of Omaha, who was also 39 years old. By 1969, Warren Buffett, who worked under Benjamin Graham, the famous value investor, and who was already a multimillionaire, listened patiently as Pappajohn pitched him on his venture capital fund. Then Warren Buffett calmly replied: "I think you're making a terrible mistake. This is not a good time for venture capitalists."

Buffett believed the market was oversold in 1969. He had liquidated his investment management partnership and took a several-year hiatus from the stock market. An interview Buffett did with *Forbes* magazine in 1974 provides insight into why he advised John Pappajohn to put a stay on starting a venture capital fund.

"Warren Buffett doesn't talk much, but when he does, it's well worth listening to. His sense of timing has been remarkable. Five years ago, late in 1969, when he was 39, he called it quits on the market. He liquidated his money management pool, Buffett Partnership, Ltd., and gave his clients their money back. Before that, in good years and bad, he had been beating the averages, making the partnership grow at a compounded annual rate of 30% before fees between 1957 and 1969 (that works out to a $10,000 investment growing to $300,000 and change).

"He quit essentially because he found the game no longer worth playing. Multiples on good stocks were sky-high, the go-go boys were 'performing' and the list was so picked over that the kind of solid bargains that Buffett likes were not to be had. He told his clients that they might do better in tax-exempt bonds than in playing the market.

"'When I got started,' he says, 'the bargains were flowing like the Johnstown flood; by 1969 it was like a leaky toilet in Altoona.' Pretty cagey, this Buffett. When all the sharp MBAs were crowding into the investment business, Buffett was quietly walking away."[2]

John Pappajohn listened respectfully to Warren Buffett, but he was not deterred in his determination to form his own venture capital fund. He forged ahead. In 1972, at the age of 44, he found and funded the company that made him a multimillionaire and became his first mega-success; coincidentally, the same year, Phil Frost took control of a healthcare company called Key Pharmaceuticals, which also marked his first mega-success.

In 1972, Pappajohn discovered Kay Laboratories, a fledgling San Diego company that had patents on chemical-reaction packs, the sport packs that are so popular today. The patents for the technology, filed in 1971, revolved around a "third material such as a form of starch which is stored in one of the compartments and which responds to the mixture of the two materials to produce a gel" (publication number US3804077, granted April 16, 1974). The chemicals that produced the gel was the essential breakthrough in the technology as it allowed the heat or cold to stay "continuously to a desired position such as the knee of a patient without having the materials in the pack slide to the opposite ends of the pack. Another advantage is that the gel prolongs the time during which the heat or cold can be applied to the desired position."

The problem was that the company was unable to get their sports packs to market. They simply did not have enough capital or salespeople to effectively penetrate the market. The company at the time was having problems meeting payroll. Pappajohn put in $100,000 of his own money and raised over $1 million to keep them afloat. In 1975, he took them public with a $4 million capital raise. Four years later, the American Hospital Supply Corporation (AHSC) acquired Kay Laboratories. American Hospital Supply "manufactured a range of products from intravenous solutions to uniforms." Pappajohn explains, "AHSC had 200 salespeople. It was a fabulous deal for them. They loved it. They said it was the best acquisition they had ever done." His stock was worth $500,000 after the transaction but he had to hold it for six months before he could sell it. The stock doubled. Still in his early 40s, he was now worth millions.

Three public companies spun out of Kay Laboratories over the next several years. The first spinoff was Medical Imaging Centers of America, which at the time was the first public rollup of MRI centers. Another one was Pancreatics, which produced an innovative insulin pump. Abbot Laboratories bought the company a few years after he took them public. His next major play was with a company called Infrasonics, which invented the first infant ventilator. The company was acquired for $66,000,000 in 1996 by Nellcor Puritan Bennett, which four years later became part of Tyco.

Next up was Urgent Care Centers of America, which IPO'd at $6.00 a share and rocketed to $48.00 in six months. RediCare ultimately acquired the company. He made tens of millions on his investment.

Several years after Kay Laboratories merged with AHSC, Pappajohn received a call from the former president of Kay Labs, Jim Sweeney. "He called me and said, 'I want to start a home healthcare company.'" Initially called Home Healthcare of America, the name would later change to Caremark. Pappajohn called Kleiner Perkins about the idea and convinced them to put the first $1 million into the company. He also put in $100,000 of his own money. In 1983, the company became the first home healthcare company in America.

> **Lesson three:** Keep an open mind. Look for things that have never been done before. The best ideas are often talked about for years before a leader emerges with the determination to get the new product or service to market. The home healthcare idea had been discussed in the healthcare industry for years, but it was Pappajohn and his team that had the vision and determination to build that company while others equally as capable never got the idea off the proverbial drawing board.

In 1987, Baxter Travenol Laboratories Inc. paid $528 million for Caremark. With his option package in Caremark, he made $18 million, in addition to making ten times his money on the stock he owned (Figure 6.1). In 2007, CVS purchased Caremark for $26.2 billion.

At this point in his career, now in his late fifties, he was worth nearly $100 million. He began investing in modern and contemporary art while continuing to start, fund, and help build companies in the healthcare space. He was elected to the board of directors of the famous modern art museum in Washington, D.C., the Hirshhorn. He was also elected to the board of directors of the National Gallery of Art. Today, he is one of the top 20 art collectors in the world. His paintings are worth an estimated $200 million.

Because RedChip is the investor relations firm for Cancer Genetics (Figure 6.2), I have had the good fortune to get to know John Pappajohn over the last 18 months. Each time I speak to him I learn something new about his life. John Pappajohn has done what the best and brightest on Wall Street have always done. He developed a network of high-net-worth individuals, venture capital funds, and microcap institutions (he is good friends with

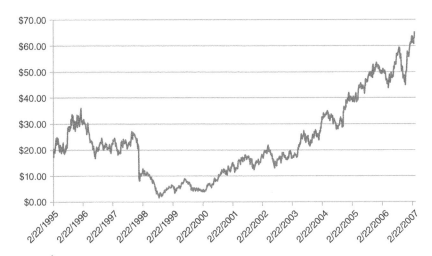

FIGURE 6.1 Caremark RX (CMX)
Data Source: Thomson Reuters Corporation.

Charles Diker, another Microcap Superstar), and spends his days hunting for small companies with promising products, technologies, and services. He has been careful to associate and work with men and women of high integrity, always carefully doing his due diligence before taking on a new project. He understands, as all the Superstars do, that to build a great company, you need and must be willing to pay for top quality talent.

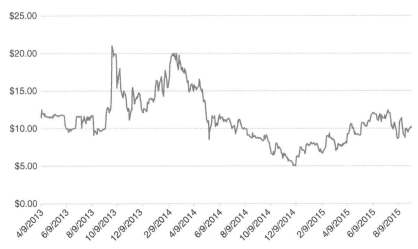

FIGURE 6.2 Cancer Genetics, Inc. (NASDAQ: CGIX)
Data Source: Thomson Reuters Corporation.

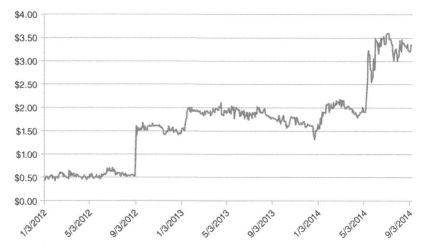

FIGURE 6.3 American CareSource Holdings (NASDAQ: ANCI)
Data Source: Thomson Reuters Corporation.

He is as active today as he has ever been. He is currently involved in the rollup of outpatient surgery centers for a company called American Care-Source Holdings (NASDAQ: ANCI; see Figure 6.3). American CareSource is the first national, publicly traded ancillary care network services company. It owns a national network of more than 4,900 ancillary service providers at more than 34,200 sites through its subsidiary, Ancillary Care Services.

He also sits on the board of CNS Response (OTCBB: CNSO), a company that has spent the past eight years developing a platform that quickly and accurately diagnoses patients for depression and other mental disorders, pinpointing the drug(s) best suited for each individual.

> Pappajohn's legacy will be large and enduring, and will transcend his work on Wall Street. He has sat on the boards of over 40 public companies, has been involved in over 100 start-ups, and has taken 50 companies public. Perhaps his most enduring legacy will be the entrepreneurial training centers he has established and funded over the past 15 years.

He has committed $30 million of his own money to these centers, of which there are now five: University of Iowa, Iowa State University, University of North Iowa, Drake, and North Iowa Area Community College.

Commenting on the entrepreneurial centers, he explains that "the intent is to train students, whether college or elementary, in how to run a business, as well as to provide advice to businesspeople across the state.

"Iowa was in desperate need of this. The centers are terribly exciting. They create success stories and empower people. Each center has its own specialty," he explains.

The University of Iowa's center focuses on engineering and health sciences. Iowa State University is focused on technologies pioneered by students and faculty from the Colleges of Agriculture, Engineering, and Veterinary Medicine. The Centers have produced over 1,000 new businesses in Iowa.

Over the years, he has gifted over $100 million to various nonprofit institutions. These contributions include not only the entrepreneurial centers, but also college scholarships for disadvantaged and high-achieving students. He donated $4 million to establish a clinical cancer center and to build a new wing at the University of Iowa hospital.

He has also been awarded honorary doctorate degrees from four universities. In 1995, he received one of the most prestigious business awards in the world, the Horatio Alger Award. The description of the Horatio Alger Award, as stated on the Horatio Alger Association website, horatioalger.org, is a fitting testimony to the life and work of John Pappajohn.

Horatio Alger Award

Members of the Association are the select few who have been honored with the Horatio Alger Award. Horatio Alger Award recipients are dedicated community leaders who demonstrate individual initiative and a commitment to excellence as exemplified by remarkable achievements accomplished through honest, hard work, self-reliance, and perseverance over adversity. All potential members must have a strong philanthropic commitment and be willing to contribute to the Association's mission: providing scholarships for highly motivated but economically disadvantaged young people.

Business Advice from John Pappajohn

- "I've made my money by being the first in markets. As a venture capitalist, you have to seek out the cutting-edge companies. You get in as early as possible. That way you make a lot more headway and profits."
- "You certainly don't make any money by being involved with mundane companies. What you do is develop a technology and then license it. That's why I'm working with the University of Iowa and Iowa State."
- "Excuses don't count. Actions speak louder than words."

- "I want to give a lot of money away. That's a main part of why I'm still working. The best way I can meet my philanthropic goals is to keep putting together good deals."
- "I've always felt life has been generous, and my philosophy has been to give back much of what I received. The logical place for me was where I got my education."
- "I've always had a dream, and this dream was to help Iowa become the most entrepreneurial state in the country. We have a great working mentality. Now all we need to do is improve our skills and have access to more capital."
- "You can't be right all the time, but you can surround yourself with honest people."

John Pappajohn Top Stock Positions

Pappajohn Capital Resources

Company	Ticker	Position (m)	Market Value ($m)
Cancer Genetics Inc.	NASDAQ: CGIX	1.34	13.70
CNS Response Inc.	OTC: CNSO	18.86	4.23
IZEA Inc.	OTC: IZEA	2.03	0.81

Source: Thomson Reuters.

Pappajohn (John G.)

Company	Ticker	Position (m)	Market Value ($m)
American CareSource Holdings Inc.	NASDAQ: ANCI	2.33	3.61
Cancer Genetics Inc.	NASDAQ: CGIX	1.52	14.68

Source: Thomson Reuters.

Notes

1. *The National Herald*, March 2, 2013, p. 16.
2. Forbes.com, *Forbes* Staff, April 30, 2008, http://www.forbes.com/2008/04/30/warren-buffett-profile-invest-oped-cx_hs_0430buffett.html.

CHAPTER 7

Byron Roth

If you want to invest in the microcap space, buy companies, not stocks; if you buy stocks, the daily fluctuations and lack of liquidity will drive you crazy.

—Byron Roth, ROTH Capital

Occupation: CEO, Owner ROTH Capital

Age: 52

Education: BBA, University of San Diego; MBA, Cornell Johnson School of Management

Estimated Net Worth: $100 million

Status: Married, eight children

Residence: Los Angeles

Nickname: "B Dazzler"

Other Business Interests: Limited partner in the Phoenix Suns

Favorite Wall Street Books: *Flash Boys*, Michael Lewis; *The Partnership*, Charles D. Ellis; *The Big Short*, Michael Lewis; *Barbarians at the Gate*, John Helyar and Bryan Burrough; *Liars Poker*, Michael Lewis

Hobbies: Yoga, hiking, biking, sports, and scouting for bands for ROTH conferences

Highly successful people usually have mentors. Growing up on a livestock farm in Iowa, Byron Roth learned the importance of hard work and discipline from his first mentor, his father. Coming from a traditional Midwestern family, the values and lessons he learned in his early years have served him well on Wall Street. He explained that his first exposure to the stock market was when he was a student at the University of San Diego, where he was part of a class project that included picking stocks. "I loved the competition. It was like competing in sports and I loved the adrenalin."

Life is full of little nudges that move us down a particular career path and Byron had several of those nudges on his way to founding ROTH Capital.

While studying for his MBA at Cornell's Johnson Graduate School of Management in 1985, Stephen Weiss, the founder of Weiss, Peck & Greer, a New York money management firm, gave a presentation on campus. After listening to Mr. Weiss speak about the financial markets, he knew then that he wanted a career on Wall Street.

While Byron was in his first year of the MBA program at Cornell, his older brother left his job at a big pharma company for the entrepreneurial world, becoming the CEO of a small public biotech company. During a break from school, his brother invited him to dinner with Marshall Swartwood, the founder of Swartwood-Hesse. Mr. Swartwood is known for giving Henry Kravis, who eventually founded KKR, his first job coming out of Columbia Business School, and ironically, he had also employed Teddy Forstmann, who later founded Forstmann & Little. Marshall's firm, Swartwood–Hesse, was the investment banker that had raised capital for Byron's brother's company, and coincidentally, Mr. Swartwood had also earned his MBA at Cornell. Through that dinner meeting, Byron secured a summer internship.

After earning his MBA in the summer of 1987, he began working full time for Swartwood-Hesse. But Black Monday hit on October 19, the same month he took his Series 7 exam. The Dow Jones Industrial Average dropped 508 points, a 22.6% decline, the biggest one-day percentage decline in the history of Wall Street. An estimated 15,000 people lost their jobs on Wall Street, including several of Byron Roth's coworkers and classmates.

His hard work, tenacity, and street smarts allowed him to keep his job at Swartwood-Hesse. Over the next several years, he would gain experience working all aspects of investment banking, generating deal flow, and helping to secure funding to close the transactions.

"I learned how to survive in a tough market and I also learned that I needed to concentrate on the revenue side of the business. In the end, nobody really cares how smart you are or where you went to school. It's all about putting points on the scoreboard," he says. One of the smartest things he did, he explains, is that early on, even though he was an investment banker, he established close relationships with institutional investors who became the sources of funding for the deals the firm generated.

In 1992, at the age of 29, Roth joined Cruttenden and Company in Southern California. Roth saw an underserved market in Southern California, as many of the new upstart successful investment banking firms were located in Northern California, feeding off the success of Silicon Valley firms such as Robertson Stephens, Hambrecht & Quist, and Montgomery Securities.

"In the early 90s," Roth explains, "there was not a microcap investment banking firm serving Southern California. We became that firm. In those days most of our deals were for companies in Southern California. It was a very good hunting ground. We discovered a lot of great companies that were under the radar screens of the Northern California firms."

When Roth joined Cruttenden, the firm was doing most of its business raising capital for private companies, he notes. Byron led the firm's efforts in building the public side of the investment banking business, generating considerable deal flow, while also establishing the investor base to fund them. In 1993, at the age of 31, he was named president of Cruttenden. In 1994, he put together a deal that would make him part owner of the firm. He bought out the venture capitalists who had invested in Cruttenden, convincing them not only to sell him their stakes, but also to finance his buyout. The skill with which he negotiated and executed that deal was a harbinger of a future that would ultimately make his firm one of the dominant investment banking firms in the microcap space.

The 1990s were strong years for Cruttenden Roth. In 1994, Roth helped put the firm on the map with the best aftermarket IPO performance for all underwriters. The firm ranked in the top 20 for aftermarket performance for five consecutive years, according to CommScan EquiDesk.

Eltron International, a Chatsworth, California–based company that made barcode labels and plastic card printers, was one of Roth's early clients.

Eltron IPO'd at a split adjusted price of $3.00 per share in 1994 with Roth as sole manager, and a follow-on offering was completed in 1995 at a split adjusted price of $10.50 per share with Robertson Stephens and Roth as managers. Eltron's stock would ultimately trade as high as $38.25 per share on December 1, 1995. In 1998, Eltron merged with Zebra Technologies (NASDAQ: ZBRA) and was eventually purchased by them for $28.62 per share. Zebra Technologies has a market cap today of $3.5 billion.

Another major win for Roth in the early days was Hansen Beverage Company, another Southern California company based in Corona, which in 2012 held 35% of the $31.9 billion energy drink market under its new name, Monster Beverage Corp. (NASDAQ: MNST), now an S&P 500 company. Roth completed a transaction for Hansen when its market capitalization was just $10 million. Today, Monster has revenue of over $2 billion and a $16 billion market capitalization (Figure 7.1).

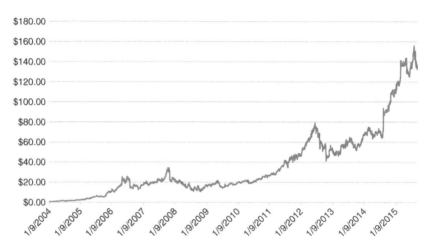

FIGURE 7.1 Monster Beverage Corporation (NASDAQ: MNST)
Data Source: Thomson Reuters Corporation.

Regarding his stock position in Hansen, he says, "I gave some of my shares to a local high school. I told them later that if they had held their stock longer they would have one of the biggest endowments in the state. I then confessed that I sold my shares too early as well. I thought I was doing great when I got out of the stock with a 10-bagger."

In 1998, Byron put together a deal to buy out the founder of Cruttenden, Walter Cruttenden, and eventually changed the name to ROTH Capital in 2000.

By the time of the buyout, the firm was gaining national recognition for its small-cap research as well as its investment banking excellence. In 2004, several ROTH Capital Partners research analysts received top honors in the *Wall Street Journal* "Best on the Street Analyst Survey," and the Forbes.com/StarMine-North American Analyst Survey. In the same year, the firm raised $1.6 billion for its clients and achieved a number one ranking for both the number of private investment in public equity (PIPE) transactions and the total dollars placed. More recently, according to Sagient Research Systems PlacementTracker, the firm has maintained a number one ranking as the most active investment bank in 2012–2013 for number of PIPE transactions.

One of the chief characteristics of the Superstars is that they tend to take risks where others will not. The equity raise the firm did for IMAX Corporation (NYSE: IMAX) in 2009 is a perfect example. While Goldman Sachs had been lead underwriter in the IPO of IMAX Corporation in 1994, it was ROTH Capital that raised $80.5 million at $7.15 a share in 2009, when the company was struggling to convert its mega-screen platform to digital.

FIGURE 7.2 IMAX Corporation (NYSE: IMAX)
Data Source: Thomson Reuters Corporation.

At the time, the co-CEO, Richard Gelfond, said, "Some people wrote us off as a dinosaur. They said, 'Until we see where IMAX is going, we don't want to do business with them.'"[1]

Roth commented on the IMAX transaction: "The big investment banks would walk by the IMAX Corporate offices on 59th Street in Manhattan and not see what we saw, an opportunity to help a struggling powerhouse with great technology." Roth helped IMAX get out from underneath its debt load. ROTH sole managed two deals just two months apart for a total of $150 million to pay off the high-yield debt.

Two years after the ROTH financing, IMAX traded in the mid-$30 range, appreciating 350%. The market cap in March 2014 was $1.77 billion (Figure 7.2).

Byron, like all the Superstars in this book, lives and breathes his business. "I am passionate about the business, so I spend a lot of my time thinking about it. I am still very involved on both the issuer side as well as the investor side of deals, helping win and execute business," he explains.

"Even though we have expanded well beyond our Southern California roots we have remained focused, and try not to be all things to all people, knowing where we can be relevant and making a difference—a lot of firms become overconfident in good markets and get too far out over their skis trying to compete where they don't have a competitive advantage and are not relevant. We've stuck to our knitting."

Since 1992, Roth and his firm have raised approximately $25 billion for smaller-cap companies, executed nearly 150 M&A transactions, and taken over 100 companies public.

Part of that knitting is doing one mega-conference every year. ROTH's 26th annual conference was March 9–12, 2014, at the Ritz Carlton in Dana Point, California. This conference is typically a four- to five-day event, drawing thousands of institutional investors and hundreds of public companies. ROTH conferences are one of the biggest, grandest events in the small-cap sector. Not only do numerous deals get done at the conference each year, the entertainment extravaganza helps to draw large institutional investors. ROTH conferences have always had world-class entertainment. Over the years, some of the biggest stars in music have performed at their conferences. "These once-a-year conferences used to be three days, and we now have events over five days. We do a charity bike ride and golf tournament. It's great because issuers, fund managers, analysts, and bankers get to spend time together at our Southern California destination conference, and the number of investment ideas generated and shared is tremendous," says Byron.

Like most of the Superstars in this book, Byron uses his wealth to help those in need. At his conference he has organized a 40-mile bicycle ride to benefit the charity organization *Challenged Athletes Foundation,* which provides support and opportunities to people with physical disabilities so they can pursue active lifestyles. Many of these athletes are troops and veterans who have suffered permanent physical injuries.

Roth has cofounded three funds, creating a recurring revenue base that has proved helpful during tough times, he explains. "Having these funds has allowed us not to do deals for survival when the markets are tough." Roth was a founder of Cortina Asset Management, EAM, and GROW, which between them manage over $4 billion in various small-cap and microcap growth strategies. As he has built his empire over the past 25 years, he notes that there have been a number of changes in the industry. "In the 1990s," he says, "there were a lot more retail firms doing transactions than there are today. The retail component was like a farm system for Roth, but that farm system lacks the vitality it did in the 1990s.

"Look at the number of IPOs in the 1990s. There were sometimes 300–400 deals a year with sub–$250 million market-cap companies but Sarbanes-Oxley, decimalization, and other factors have contributed to a slowdown among IPOs for smaller companies." Roth believes the JOBS Act will help bring back the market for microcap IPOs.

Byron Roth is still relatively young in comparison to the elder statesmen of the Superstar Club. ROTH Capital continues to be a dominant player in the microcap space and we would do well to follow his career and his firm. He is a member of the University of San Diego Board of Trustees and a Founding Member of the Executive Cabinet for the Athletic Department. He is also a member of the Advisory Council for the Samuel Curtis Johnson Graduate School of Management at Cornell University, and the Executive Board of SMU's Cox School of Business.

Byron Roth's Advice to Microcap Investors in His Own Words

1. "You can be happy with the companies you own, but may not be happy with their stock performance. If you know what you're investing in and are patient, you'll have your day when the market recognizes the value, but that may not be today or tomorrow."

2. "Management is the key asset of a great company, particularly in small companies with limited resources. Bet on the team shaping the strategy and executing on the business."

3. "Investing can be really hard just before it gets easy . . . but it can also be really easy just before it gets hard . . . don't get too full of yourself when things are good and don't get too down on yourself when things are bad."

4. "Knowing when to sell a winner can be a very elusive skill. It often makes sense to keep a small percentage of the shares for idiot's insurance."

5. "Know why a company is valued as a microcap, and how it got there . . . whether you are just early, the stock is a fallen angel, the company has balance sheet issues or poor execution . . . then figure out how it will break out of microcap-land. If you can't figure out how it will get to the next level, then don't buy the stock."

6. "When no one wants these stocks is the best time to buy them."

Note

1. David Lieberman, "IMAX Makes a Dramatic Comeback," *USA Today*, May 10, 2008.

CHAPTER 8

Charles Diker

Do your homework, understand companies you invest in forwards and backwards.

—Charles Diker, Diker Management

Occupation: Investment Manager, Diker Management

Money Under Management: $600 million

Age: 82

Education: Bachelor of Arts, Harvard University, 1956; MBA, Harvard, 1958

Estimated Net Worth: $700 million

Status: Married to Valerie Diker, three children

Primary Residence: Manhattan

NickName: "The Private One"

Born in Brooklyn in 1934, Charles Diker comes from a family of businessmen. Schooled early in the art of trade, his parents owned a successful fashion accessory manufacturing and distribution business in Manhattan. He was an academic high achiever in middle and high school, earning a seat in the world's most elite institution of higher learning, and at the time, the best business school in the country. In 1956, he graduated with honors, earning a bachelor of arts in Business from Harvard. Three years later he graduated with an MBA from the Harvard Graduate School of Business.

It is worth noting that Charles Diker attended Harvard during the same period that the Ford Foundation was making what it called "the big push" to raise the quality of education in business schools across America. The

Ford Foundation, in the 1950s, had designated Harvard Business School as a center of excellence and a model for all business schools in America. The grants would help pay the salaries of some of the sharpest business minds in academia and result in a plethora of research on business strategy, financial models, and most important, management theory.

In the 1950s, business and government leaders were focused on building upon the lessons learned in America's World War II industrialization. A focus on management, and, in particular, strategic management as a discipline was an important theme during this era (see Alfred Chandler, *Strategy and Structure*,[1] and Peter Drucker, *The Practice of Management*[2]).

During Diker's formative years at Harvard, four core ideas were being taught in business management classes: the importance of developing a long-term strategic plan; developing strategic objectives that are communicated throughout the organization; creating work environments that encouraged communication and collaboration among employees and departments; and the importance of finding the best and brightest to help lead an organization.

During 1953–1964, the Ford Foundation granted $5.2 million (equivalent to $41.4 million in today's dollars) to Harvard Business School, more grant money than was given to any other business school in the country.[3]

In 1960, Diker leveraged his quick mind and Ivy League MBA and launched his business career as the assistant to the founder and president of Revlon, Charles Revson. Revlon had IPO'd only three years earlier on the NYSE with a market capitalization of $500 million. Revson started Revlon in 1932 at the age of 28. By the time Diker arrived at the company, Revson was 56 years old, and becoming recognized as a brand merchandising genius. Revson is considered the father of the art of "modern branding."

Diker could not have chosen a better training ground for his future career in the capital markets. Revlon, at the time, was a fast-growing company in a very competitive industry led by a high-energy, hard-charging, no-nonsense leader. Revson was a mentor to Diker, and they forged a lifelong friendship and business relationship. Diker learned the science of merchandising, packaging, and branding from Revson. "He taught me the importance of perfection; in creating and building a brand, everything has to be just right. It starts with the product. If the product is not right, the branding won't matter," says Diker. While Diker was working for the company, Revlon launched one of the bestselling perfumes of all time, called, not coincidentally, "Charlie."

He also learned from Revson how to run a company with the proverbial iron fist. Revson was known for operating with an extreme eye for detail and for getting things right the first time. He had a low tolerance for mediocrity and a high regard for discipline, clear thinking, hard work, and intelligence, which Diker had in abundance.

Diker's training under Revson's no-nonsense management style is perhaps best illustrated by the following famous statement the founder of Revlon once made to one of his lieutenants: "Look, kiddie. I built this business by being a bastard. I run it by being a bastard. I'll always be a bastard, and don't you ever try to change me."[4]

In 1967, Diker, now one of Revson's most trusted and able lieutenants, became the vice president of marketing. His leadership, strategic vision, and intelligence was recognized not only by Revson but by other business leaders. After spending nine years at Revlon and now 34 years old, a toymaker named Aurora recruited him to become the youngest CEO of a major toy company.

In 1968, Aurora was one of the dominant toy manufacturers in the country, achieving iconic status as the makers of plastic model kits: dinosaurs, King Kong, Tarzan, and its much-maligned tortured figures model kits. He ran the company for six years, applying the branding and leadership skills he learned at Revlon. In 1971, under his leadership, he helped put together a merger with Nabisco, the same year the food conglomerate reached $1 billion in sales.

After he left Aurora, he became a limited partner at Weiss Peck and Greer, a money management fund focused on smaller-cap stocks. In his early 40s, he became involved with a number of small, fast-growing companies, including Neutrogena, which was sold to Johnson & Johnson for $935 million in 1994. He sat on the board of directors of over 10 companies, including Slim-Fast, the diet food company, which began in 1977 as a product line of the Thompson Medical Company.

Already a millionaire by the time he was 36, Diker entered his 30s during a time of rapid economic growth in America. The Kennedy tax cuts, the Vietnam War, and the growth of the manufacturing sector would contribute to a doubling of the gross domestic product "measured in current dollars" from 1960 to 1970.[5]

In the 1960s Diker began investing in stocks, learning the market, and developing an investment approach that would make him hundreds of millions over the next 40 years.

In 1986, at the age of 51, Diker, already a seasoned and highly respected Wall Street professional, became chairman of the board of Stendig Industries, a company in Little Falls, New Jersey, that had its origins in a company founded in 1946 in Toronto, Canada, which sold 35 mm cameras and other optical products.

That company would eventually evolve into Cantel Medical (NYSE: CMN). In 1963, while Diker was still vice president of Marketing at Revlon, the company went public. Twenty-three years later, Diker was appointed chairman of the board. When he joined the company sales were less than $40 million. The company was losing money and had a substantial amount of debt. The company lacked a long-term strategic vision and a clear path to profitability and was badly in need of new leadership. Diker and CEO James Reilly realized that their distribution agreement with Olympus Optical was their "most valuable asset." One of its most important products at the time was endoscopes. Their acquisition of MediVators, Inc.. in 1996, a company that sold equipment that disinfected endoscopes, a product that had received FDA approval only two years earlier, marked a key turning point for the company. MediVators became the basis of Cantel Medical, which in 1996 was generating only $3 million in revenue.

> Under Diker's leadership, the company repositioned its business. In 1988, he and the new CEO, James P. Reilly, a seasoned executive whose previous position was president and chief operating officer of the North American Watch Company, began shedding its furniture assets and other non-medical-related businesses.

By 1999, the company was back at $50 million in revenue, but this time with a more focused product line and profitability. By 2004, sales had grown to $170 million with almost $11 million in net income. The company was named to the *Forbes* list of top 100 small companies in America in 2012 and 2013.

In fiscal 2013, the company reported revenue of $410 million and $29 million net income. In January 2014, they acquired Sterilator Company, Inc. For fiscal 2014, Cantel reported record revenue of $488 million and record net income of $44.1 million. The market cap of Cantel Medical today is $2.2 billion. Big companies start small. Diker currently personally owned 5.2 million shares of Cantel Medical valued at $200 million as of October 2014.

The company is a leader in infection prevention and control products for the healthcare industry and continues to make strategic acquisitions. In 2002, Diker and his son Mark founded Diker Management, an investment management firm. "The firm focuses on global microcap and small-cap equities but has the flexibility to invest internationally and across the capitalization spectrum. Diker makes multiyear investments in innovating companies that are both under-followed and inefficiently priced by the investment community. It conducts intensive fundamental research with the goal of creating superior long-term risk adjusted investment returns."[6] The fund's net assets are approximately $600 million. I will note the fund holds a position in Cancer Genetics (NASDAQ: CGIX), a RedChip client company.

Diker's list of accomplishments runs deep. Diker has been a director of BeautiControl Inc., a subsidiary of Tupperware, since 1987, where he has been instrumental in helping them brand their in-home spa products.

He has sat on the board of several public and private companies, including Lowes Corp., AMF Bowling, and Carolina Group.

Like the other elder statesmen in this book, Charles Diker owns an extensive collection of modern and European art, and he is also the founding chairman of the National Museum of the American Indian, and owns a large collection of American Indian Art, which has been displayed at the Smithsonian Institution. In 2012, he was elected to the board of trustees of the Solomon R. Guggenheim Foundation. He has also served on the boards of the Smithsonian Institution and St. John's College, and is a trustee at the Mailman School of Public Health of Columbia University.

Diker's Key Principles of Investing in His Own Words

1. "Invest in companies whose businesses you can understand" (many of his biggest successes were in consumer product companies, a space he knew well from his time spent at Revlon).
2. "Get to know management, look for intelligence, a high level of integrity, strong communication skills and make sure they understand their products and business well."
3. "The company must have a niche product or service and you must believe in that niche."
4. "Patience is important. Remember, you are not buying a stock, you are buying a company. You may have to hold it for 10 years before it matures into a major homerun."
5. "Do your homework, understand companies you invest in forwards and backwards."

Charles Diker Top Stock Positions

Diker (Charles M)

Company	Ticker	Position (m)	Market Value ($m)
Cantel Medical Corp..	NYSE: CMN	5.62	301.60
Loews Corp..	NYSE: L	0.00	0.13

Source: Thomson Reuters Corporation.

Diker Management, LLC

Company	Ticker	Position (m)	Market Value ($m)
Smith Micro Software Inc.	NASDAQ: SMSI	4.39	5.04
Cantel Medical Corp.	NYSE: CMN	2.05	109.81
Cyren Ltd.	NASDAQ: CYRN	1.98	3.74
Allot Communications Ltd.	NASDAQ: ALLT	1.84	13.26
YuMe Inc.	NYSE: YUME	1.81	9.81
Mattersight Corp.	NASDAQ: MATR	1.36	8.00
IZEA Inc.	OTC: IZEA	1.18	0.47
Crossroads Systems Inc.	NASDAQ: CRDS	1.13	1.74
Attunity Ltd.	NASDAQ: ATTU	1.03	13.53
Jive Software Inc.	NASDAQ: JIVE	1.01	5.31
Magic Software Enterprises Ltd.	NASDAQ: MGIC	0.99	6.55
RR Media Ltd.	NASDAQ: RRM	0.97	7.32
Sapiens International Corporation NV	NASDAQ: SPNS	0.97	10.10
Adept Technology Inc.	NASDAQ: ADEP	0.91	6.52
ShoreTel Inc.	NASDAQ: SHOR	0.89	6.05
Chegg Inc.	NYSE: CHGG	0.85	6.68
Selectica Inc.	NASDAQ: SLTC	0.85	3.66
Silver Spring Networks Inc.	NYSE: SSNI	0.80	9.96
GigOptix Inc.	NYSE: GIG	0.69	1.18
Apple Inc.	NASDAQ: AAPL	0.64	80.51
Carbonite Inc.	NASDAQ: CARB	0.62	7.29
Ikanos Communications Inc.	NASDAQ: IKAN	0.60	1.24
ID Systems Inc.	NASDAQ: IDSY	0.59	3.60
TechTarget Inc.	NASDAQ: TTGT	0.59	5.26
Onvia Inc.	NASDAQ: ONVI	0.50	2.16
Radware Ltd.	NASDAQ: RDWR	0.50	11.00
LivePerson Inc.	NASDAQ: LPSN	0.41	4.02
American Apparel Inc.	NYSE: APP	0.39	0.19
Care.com Inc.	NYSE: CRCM	0.36	2.16
Rosetta Stone Inc.	NYSE: RST	0.34	2.74
Camtek Ltd.	NASDAQ: CAMT	0.31	0.88
Yodlee Inc.	NASDAQ: YDLE	0.31	4.46
Support.com Inc.	NASDAQ: SPRT	0.29	0.41
bebe stores Inc.	NASDAQ: BEBE	0.26	0.52
TheStreet Inc.	NASDAQ: TST	0.24	0.44
Rackspace Hosting Inc.	NYSE: RAX	0.23	8.73
Dominion Diamond Corp.	NYSE: DDC	0.22	3.08
Synchronoss Technologies Inc.	NASDAQ: SNCR	0.22	9.87
EVINE Live Inc.	NASDAQ: EVLV	0.21	0.56
Tremor Video Inc.	NYSE: TRMR	0.19	0.55

Company	Ticker	Position (m)	Market Value ($m)
Summer Infant Inc.	NASDAQ: SUMR	0.18	0.35
New York & Company Inc.	NYSE: NWY	0.17	0.46
Electronics for Imaging Inc.	NASDAQ: EFII	0.17	7.46
Axalta Coating Systems Ltd.	NYSE: AXTA	0.16	5.30
Christopher & Banks Corp.	NYSE: CBK	0.15	0.60
Spark Networks Inc.	NYSE: LOV	0.15	0.45
iShares US Home Construction ETF	NYSE: ITB	0.13	3.54
Burlington Stores Inc.	NYSE: BURL	0.12	6.33
NXP Semiconductors NV	NASDAQ: NXPI	0.12	11.65
PRGX Global Inc.	NASDAQ: PRGX	0.12	0.52

Source: Thomson Reuters Corporation.

Notes

1. Alfred D. Chandler, Jr., *Strategy and Structure: Chapters in the History of the American Industrial Enterprise* (Cambridge, MA: MIT Press, 1962).
2. Peter F. Drucker, *The Practice of Management* (New York: Harper & Row, 1954).
3. Rakesh Khurana, *From Higher Aims to Hired Hands: The Social Transformation of American Business Schools and the Unfulfilled Promise of Management as a Profession* (Princeton, NJ: Princeton University Press, 2010).
4. "New Hampshire People: Charles Revson," *New Hampshire Union Leader*, April 6, 2013.
5. Ross Gregory, *Cold War America, 1946 to 1990* (New York: Facts on File, 2003): 69.
6. *Street Insider*, August 7, 2014.

CHAPTER 9

Phil Sassower

Work hard, be a long-term thinker, develop tenacity and remember nothing happens without taking calculated risks.

—Phil Sassower, Phoenix Group

Occupation: Venture Capitalist; President, Phoenix Group; Chairman, CEO of Xplore (NASDAQ: XPLR)

Age: 75

Estimate Net Worth: $500 million

Residence: New York, NY

Education: BSc in Business, Queens College, 1961; Harvard Law School, 1964

Favorite Books: "I did all my reading as a lawyer."

At age 74, Phil Sassower has the energy of a much younger man. He is tall, vibrant, and fit, and very much a family man. His office credenza is full of family pictures. He is president of the Phoenix Group, a family office that has served as an investment vehicle and talent pool for the companies he has invested in and helped build over the past 40 years. His sons, Robert and Mark, are vice presidents.

As a contemporary of Charles Diker, it's interesting to note that his father was also a wealthy clothing merchant in New York. With both a legal and accounting background, his skillset is well-suited for the capital markets. He, like Phil Frost and Charles Diker, was educated in the Ivy League. After earning his bachelor degree in Business and Accounting at

Queens University, graduating with honors, he was accepted into Harvard Law School, where he earned his law degree in 1964.

Sassower had the good fortune to marry into a prominent Wall Street family. In 1964, after graduating from Harvard Law, he went to work for Oppenheimer & Company, a New York investment banking firm founded in 1950 by his father-in-law, Max E. Oppenheimer. "This was during the days of Leon Levy," he explains. Both Max Oppenheimer and Leon Levy were highly regarded leaders on Wall Street in the 1960s. Levy became a partner in Oppenheimer in 1956 and co-founded the Oppenheimer Funds. *Forbes* magazine once called Leon Levy a "Wall Street investment genius." His book, *The Mind of Wall Street*, is a captivating history of Wall Street and provides a broad sweep of the trends and personalities that defined it from the 1960s through 2002.

Levy makes the point in his book that Oppenheimer was one of the first firms to systematically cover smaller-cap stocks. Max Oppenheimer sometimes invested in Phil's deals and also provided guidance when needed. In 1969, Sassower left Oppenheimer and started his own brokerage firm, Sassower, Jacobs, and Schneider, which later became a public company called Arc Equities, an entity he would later use as a vehicle to merge into a company that would make him rich.

In the beginning, his brokerage firm first functioned, to use his own words, as participating investment bankers, but after 15 or 20 deals, "we asked ourselves: 'Why raise money for these companies?' Let's put in our own money and our friends and family, and take an active role in helping build and sell them." He describes himself as an "agnostic value player" and makes it clear that he has never been a deal junkie. Throughout his 45-year career he has been closely involved with only about 10 companies.

Sassower began his business career during a time when venture capitalism as an industry was just beginning to emerge. The Small Business Investment Act of 1958 officially allowed the U.S. Small Business Administration (SBA) to help finance and manage smaller, emerging growth entrepreneurial businesses. During the 1960s and 1970s, venture capital firms focused their investment activity primarily on starting and expanding companies. More often than not, these companies were exploiting breakthroughs in electronic, medical, or data-processing technology. As a result, venture capital came to be almost synonymous with technology finance."[1]

While Phil Frost, Charles Diker, and John Pappajohn (Microcap Superstars) made hundreds of millions with companies in the medical and healthcare industries, Sassower made his first $50 million by investing in and restructuring a textiles manufacturing company.

At age 31, Sassower discovered Bates Manufacturing, a textile manufacturer founded in 1850 in Lewiston, Maine. In the 1950s, Bates was Maine's largest employer but by the late 1960s the company was carrying a heavy debt load and losing money. The textile industry was increasingly under pressure from Asian textile manufacturers, including China, who were selling into the U.S. market at cutthroat prices. Listed on the NYSE, the stock had fallen to around $12 a share.

Sassower, who learned about the company from one of his friends, stepped in and structured a convertible debenture to relieve their debt. Over the next four years, he got deeply involved in the company, ultimately becoming its largest shareholder and its CEO. His group invested $8 million at $10.00 a share. The company began manufacturing and selling high-quality bedspreads in the early 1970s, as this was a product for which there was high demand and strong profit margins. He also rolled in a substantial coal asset, which proved to be a brilliant and very profitable strategic move. "We bought the coal company," he states, "as a play to hedge ourselves against the costs of the synthetic material Bates was buying to make its textiles." His team paid $10 million ($10 per share) for Virginia Iron Coal and Coke, which owned low sulfur coal assets. They then leased those assets to Pickens and other coal mining companies that paid them a royalty based on the amount of coal they mined.

The 1973 oil embargo, while wreaking havoc on the U.S. economy, was a major boon for their coal asset and Bates Manufacturing.

Curtis E. Harvey, in his book, *Coal in Appalachia: An Economic Analysis*, sums up the impact of the Arab embargo on the coal industry: "Historically, the welfare of the coal industry has closely paralleled fluctuations in the price of petroleum and, therefore, the welfare of the oil industry. The price of coal moves in the same direction as the price of petroleum, albeit at a lower level and with a time lag. This so-called price tracking occurs because when the price of oil rises, coal becomes an increasingly attractive substitute. Market demand increases tend to raise the price of coal; abatement of demand tends to reduce it."

The book explains that "after the unexpected Arab actions, however, the price of coal, in particular the spot-market price, rose because embargo restrictions reduced sharply the available oil supplies and because the price of imported oil had increased fivefold. Uncertainties concerning the future availability of adequate supplies of imported oil, coupled with sharply higher prices, generated a strong upward shift in demand for its most suitable substitute: coal. The price of coal rose dramatically."[2]

Coal did rise dramatically to $40.00 a ton in 1974, which meant that the Bates coal acquisition was generating income of $1 million a month, a 10-fold increase. Sassower's timing on purchasing the coal asset was impeccably fortuitous. In 1977, Sassower's group sold the coal company to American

Natural Resources. They also sold the textile business. They netted $72.00 a share for an investment in which they paid $10.00 a share, a 700% profit. Not quite 40 years old, he was now worth nearly $50 million.

Another investment that generated hundreds of millions in profits for his group was Newpark Resources (NYSE: NR), which he funded at $0.20 a share. The company was incorporated as New Park Mining in 1932 but changed its name to Newpark Resources in 1972. In 1977, it listed on the New York Stock Exchange but was delisted in 1986 after it sold off one of its divisions to a bank to relieve its debt load. This is around the time that Sassower took an interest in the company. The company began a restructuring in 1986. In 1987, Sassower's group invested $10 million. The company refocused its business and became a major player in hazardous waste cleanup. Again, Sassower had the foresight to redirect the company into a fast growing industry. Remember, the late president Richard M. Nixon established the Environmental Protection Agency in 1970. New tougher environmental regulations in the 1970s mandated the cleanup and restoration of hazardous waste sites. In 1991, Newpark listed on the NASDAQ and then four years later as revenue topped $80 million it listed again on the NYSE (Figure 9.1).

Adjusted for splits and dividends, the price of Newpark Resources reached $105.00 per share in the mid-1990s. The Phoenix Group made $200 million on their "calculated risk play." Newpark Resources' 2013 revenue was $1.1 billion with $65.3 million in net income. The company is a leading international oil services company with three major divisions: drilling fluids; mats and integrated services; and environmental services.

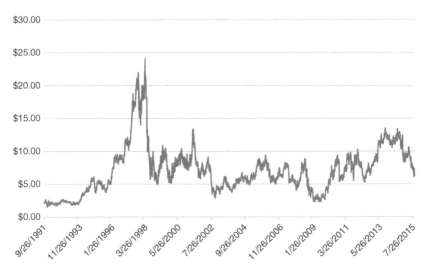

FIGURE 9.1 Newpark Resources (NYSE: NR)
Data Source: Thomson Reuters Corporation.

Even the best of the Superstars make mistakes and put their capital and resources into companies that for reasons beyond their control do not turn out as planned. Case in point: Tesero Oil, a NYSE company, with operations in Alaska.

Here's how Sassower explains the failure of Tesero Oil.

The stock was undervalued because it had the cloud of a Department of Energy investigation hanging over it for violating rules on pricing. We looked closely at the company, the management, the assets, and the business model and realized it was incredibly undervalued. We believed the investigation would not lead to any serious trouble for the company, as during the 1980s many oil and gas companies were being investigated on the basis of regulatory issues related to pricing. We believed it was a political thing that would blow over. The problem was, we put $15 million in the company, but we couldn't get a bank to give them debt financing. We simply couldn't get a deal done. We couldn't get Tesero properly financed. The lesson for us was not to get involved in giant companies dependent on banks and third parties. We wanted to buy the entire company and take it public. The banks thought the liability would be too painful. Ultimately, all these companies settled with the Department of Energy. We sold our stock and got out.

During my interview, Sassower keeps coming back to Xplore Technologies (NASDAQ: XPLR), a company that makes rugged computers. He first invested in the company in 2004 when it was a penny stock listed on the Toronto stock exchange. Though the company floundered for years, he saw something in their technology that excited him.

"This computer is the most rugged computer on the planet. The U.S. Army tested it. They dropped it from 50 feet, they dragged it behind a truck. It's the toughest mobile computer out there and the market for this technology is enormous. Think about it. Police departments, the military, telephone line repairmen, they all need a computer that's durable, waterproof, and shockproof. It's important to be in the right place at the right time in order to capitalize on the business," he says enthusiastically, "and that's where we are today with Xplore."

He continues: "The story is now unfolding the way I imagined it." In 2013, the company listed on the NASDAQ and raised $10 million. For the three months ending June 30, 2014, Xplore reported revenue of $8,267,000, compared to $5,856,000 for the three months ending June 30, 2013, an increase of 40% (Figure 9.2). Sales to the U.S. military have increased substantially and the company is very close to reaching net profitability.

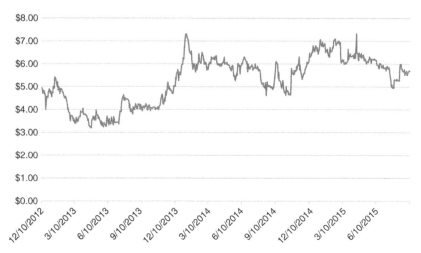

FIGURE 9.2 Xplore Technologies (NASDAQ: XPLR)
Data Source: Thomson Reuters Corporation.

Sassower continues to play a major role at Xplore Technologies. He is a hands-on investor, a long-term player. Like most of the Superstars in this book, he has made his fortune discovering companies that on the surface looked as though they were mediocre at best. The Superstars, however, go deeper and see things that others miss. With Xplore, he saw a technology that though still not commercialized, could, if properly capitalized, emerge as a leader in a multibillion-dollar rugged computer market. Though the market cap still does not reflect the true value of the company according to Sassower, the growth in sales suggests his investment appears to be working.

Lessons from Phil Sassower
- "Nothing happens without calculated risk. To be successful in any business, and particularly microcaps, you have to work hard, develop long-term thinking, and learn tenacity."
- "Business is one part knowledge, one part luck."
- "When I get involved in a company, I fund it initially through my own money and friends and family and the first question I ask is: 'Does the concept make sense?' That's where I start."
- "You may have to work 10 years on a company to make it successful and achieve a healthy return on your investment."
- "Companies are like humans; they get knocked down, fall behind, the best ones get back up, and go for the rebound. Some make it, some don't. You've got to have the fortitude to see it through."

Phil Sassower Top Stock Positions

SG Phoenix Ventures LLC

Company	Ticker	Position (m)	Market Value ($m)
Communication Intelligence Corp.	OTC: CICI	61.13	1.52
Xplore Technologies Corp.	NASDAQ: XPLR	1.22	7.77

Source: Thomson Reuters Corporation.

Notes

1. Jake Powers, "The History of Private Equity & Venture Capital," Corporate LiveWire, February 20, 2012.
2. Curtis E. Harvey, *Coal in Appalachia: An Economic Analysis* (Lexington, KY: University Press of Kentucky, 1986), p. 133.

CHAPTER 10

Barry Honig

I had grown tired of backing make-believe CEOs and entrepreneurs, so my partners and I went on the board, took a hands-on approach, built the company, and put in a solid management team, then sold the company to Yahoo. [In 2011, Yahoo purchased Interclick for $270 million.]

—Barry Honig, GRQ Consultants

Occupation: Financier, Entrepreneur, Investor

Age: 44

Education: BSc in Business, George Washington University

Estimated Net Worth: $200 million

Status: Married, four children

Residence: Boca Raton, FL; 10,000-square-foot home on the Boca Bay

Nickname: "The Machine"

Hobbies: Exercise, reading, work

Favorite Stock: Pershing Gold (NASDAQ: PGLC)

Part promoter, investor, financier, entrepreneur, and deal maker, Barry Honig is the most active microcap player on the Street today. At age 43, he is still relatively young, and if he continues at his current pace, he could reach billionaire status before he reaches the age of 50. He is the youngest of the Superstars. He began his career on Wall Street in the late 1990s, working as a trader for Ramius, specializing in distressed equities, arbitrage, and long/ short strategies.

Realizing he could make more money investing in and restructuring deals, in 2004, at the age of 32, he started GRQ Consultants, Inc.

He began learning the financial markets early. Influenced by his father, a CPA and entrepreneur, Barry began reading the *Wall Street Journal* and *New York Times* at the age of 13.

There is no one in the microcap space whom I have met who operates at his pace. Feared by some, hated by others, over the last six years his career has skyrocketed. Few play the microcap game as well as Honig. The CEO of Pershing Gold (NASDAQ: PGLC), a company Barry founded and financed, summed it up well when he said to me: "Barry outworks everyone else and is always two steps ahead of everyone as well."

The intensity with which he approaches his work combined with his street smarts and ability to evaluate a business and its management is considered by some ruthless, others brilliant. But he is a machine, and he will cut to the heart of a matter in minutes. The bottom line for him is results. He is a tough negotiator. You do not get into his inner circle unless you execute at a high level, and you do not stay in if you are not consistently performing at a high level.

He is married with four children. His priorities in life are narrow and focused: family and work. "In my free time, I read papers, spend time with my wife and kids, work out, exercise; I don't watch TV. I like what I do. Work is my hobby, I don't know how to relax."

Worth approximately $200 million, Barry lives in Boca Raton, Florida, in a 10,000-square-foot walled compound on the Boca Raton bay, a 50-foot yacht parked just off his expansive back patio.

He invests in anything that makes sense, and he takes big pieces of companies at very cheap prices.

> "The key is management; if you don't have the right management team, forget it, nothing matters more in small companies," he says, echoing the thoughts of all the Superstars in this book.

The first time I met Barry Honig was in 2008 in Las Vegas. He requested a meeting primarily because he was familiar with RedChip's investor relations work for ZAGG, Inc. (NASDAQ: ZAGG). While RedChip was the investor relations firm, the stock had appreciated from $0.73 on the OTC Bulletin Board to $7.00 with a listing on the NASDAQ. In fact, RedChip was the first firm to put research coverage on ZAGG. Ultimately the stock reached a high of $14.50 (Figure 10.1). Barry was a passive investor in the company.

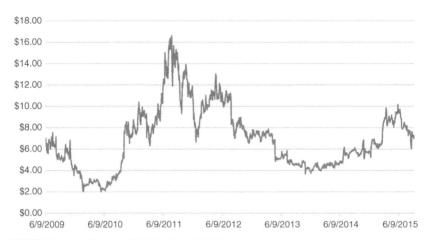

FIGURE 10.1 ZAGG Inc. (NASDAQ: ZAGG)
Data Source: Thomson Reuters Corporation.

I was dressed in a suit and tie, hot and sweaty, while Barry was wearing shorts and a tank top, tanned and buff, when we met in a cabana by the pool at the Wynn Hotel. I was there for a conference, and he was vacationing with his wife and family for a few days. He was working on several deals, as he always is, and had two to show me, both of which I was hoping to get as investor relations clients. At the time, his hottest deal was a company called Interclick, which was trading at around $2.00, a company he founded along with Michael Brauser and funded in 2006 (more later on Interclick and how he made $22 million on the deal). We sat in the cabana, ordered a couple of drinks, and he proceeded to grill me with questions about RedChip.

"You're the hottest IR firm on the Street right now, aren't you?," he asked. "Tell me about your model." Trying to sound modest, I answered, "We're working on it."

I went on to differentiate our platform by emphasizing the fact that we use a multimedia approach, combining research, print mail, conferences, telemarketing, social media, roadshows, and radio (at the time we did not have a TV show). While we were talking, four or five calls came in. He takes one, chats for a few minutes, and ignores the rest.

The Interclick Story

"All right," he says, "I've got two deals right now for you. One is called Interclick. I have another IR firm working it right now, but I may bring on another firm. I like having two or three firms working my deals. Stock's going to $7.00–$10.00. Really, I don't need you on it, but I'll think about it."

Interclick is an Internet technology company that developed a platform that optimizes and predicts online audience behaviors, integrating analytics to customize digital campaigns in a way that was more precise and granular than any technology at the time. Barry and a couple of friends brainstormed the idea for Interclick and then put together the funding and management team.

"I and a couple of my associates founded Interclick in 2006. It was a combination of three companies in the Internet advertising space. Dr. Phil Frost was also an investor in the company. Annual revenue grew from $2 million to over $100 million in only three years.

"Prior to Interclick," he explains, "I was involved in an Internet company which I raised $40 million for. The CEO I backed was a bad guy, investors lost their entire $40 million. Relationships are important, I had investors to take care of so I wanted to come back strong. I wanted to redeem myself."

I had grown tired of backing make-believe CEOs and entrepreneurs, so my partners and I went on the board, took a hands-on approach, put in a solid management team. We fired the CEO and CFO of the previous company, bought all their stock from them, and financed the company. Revenue went from about $200,000 a month to almost $10 million a month in less than three years. We went from five employees to 75 employees and six offices around the country.

In November 2011, Interclick announced that Yahoo was acquiring the company for $270 million, or $9.00 a share, a 22% premium to its then market price. Barry was cochairman of the company. He made approximately $22 million on the transaction (Figure 10.2).

FIGURE 10.2 Interclick (NASDAQ: ICLK)
Data Source: Thomson Reuters Corporation.

A *Wall Street Journal* article, "Yahoo Buys Interclick for $270 Million," describes their reasoning behind the acquisition:

> *The acquisition is meant to solve what has been a chronic problem for Yahoo: digital-ad sellers buying up ad space on Yahoo websites and selling it to advertisers for a much higher price. Yahoo has thus been losing out on tens of millions of dollars in revenue a year or more, industry experts say.*
>
> *With Interclick, Yahoo will have better data to understand what its ad space is worth and sell it for a higher price through an automated system.*[1]

For Honig, the key lesson in this deal was that "your reputation is all you have. Stay loyal to your investors. Good things can come out of bad situations, particularly in smaller caps. And again, management is the key."

The next time I spoke to Barry was four years later in the spring of 2012, when we were representing a company called ChromaDex (OTCQB: CDXC). ChromaDex is a natural products company that develops and acquires proprietary-based ingredient technologies used in nutritional supplements, foods, beverages, pharmacological products, and cosmetics. The company has partnered with leading research institutions. Barry is the chairman of the board. He is also an investor in the company and has helped them raise more than $15 million over the past four years.

As the chairman, and the one who has raised most of the money for ChromaDex, Barry has a significant interest in ensuring its investor relations dollars are giving the company a positive return. Though the company is not yet profitable, it has developed a war chest of patented ingredients such as Niagin™, a next-generation Vitamin B3; and PUREENERGY™, a combination of caffeine and pTeroPure, "a novel, next-generation, functional caffeine alternative."

After grilling me on what we had done for ChromaDex as their investor relations firm for the past 12 months, Barry referred another company to RedChip, called MusclePharm (OTCQB: MSLP).

The Story of MusclePharm

The story of how Barry helped turn around MusclePharm serves as another primer on how Honig has a knack for restructuring companies for success when they are failing in the capital markets. MusclePharm is a sports nutrition company founded by ex-NFL player Brad Pyatt. Started out of Pyatt's garage seven years ago, the company experienced triple-digit annual revenue growth during 2009–2012, but was financing itself through toxic convertible debentures. These debentures allowed investors to convert debt into stock and then reset the price they could convert, at increasingly lower prices, a way of financing that is devastating to the stock price and dramatically increases dilution.

When Barry Honig got involved the stock was trading at $0.005 per share. As an athlete and weightlifter, Barry began using their products, liked them, and after doing his homework contacted the company. Realizing the company had the potential to be a dominant player in its space but needed to raise capital and restructure its debt, he invested $2 million of his own money and raised an additional $8 million.

Barry also convinced Microcap Superstar Dr. Phil Frost to invest $2 million. After raising the capital, the company executed a 500:1 reverse stock split to $5.25 in December 2012. RedChip became the investor relations firm shortly after, and I first featured them on my TV show in February 2013 at $5.75. Four months later, the stock reached a new all-time-high of $12.50.

In September 2014, the stock hit another all-time-high of $14.10. They have signed endorsement deals with Arnold Schwarzenegger and Johnny Manziel. MusclePharm is also an official sponsor of the Ultimate Fighting Championship.

The stock has fallen to a $65 million market cap (as of September 8, 2015), primarily because they have not hit their earnings target, as losses have been substantial over the last nine months. Revenue for the first six months of fiscal 2015 was $91.7 million, with losses of $14.5 million. Also weighing on the stock was an SEC investigation involving the lack of full disclosure of certain executive compensation. But the MusclePharm story is a classic turnaround. Investors who bought after the restructuring, when the stock was trading in the $5–$7 range, had an opportunity for a 100% return on investment in less than six months, but the stock today is trading at $4.75. Those investors who bought at higher levels and did not sell on the way down may be suffering large losses. Again, MusclePharm is typical of many microcap stocks that run up on good news or rumor of good news, only to come falling back, potentially presenting another buying opportunity.

The lesson here is that there are companies with great products but that have failed to properly maneuver the often frenetic and volatile small-cap financial markets. A company can linger for years in relative obscurity, and then come to life with the right partners, management, and financing structure.

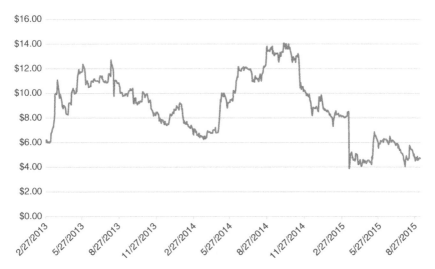

FIGURE 10.3 MusclePharm (OTCQB: MSLP)
Data Source: Thomson Reuters Corporation.

The Story of Pershing Gold

Pershing Gold (NASDAQ: PGLC) is Barry's most important company, one that he is determined to make work for his investors. The story behind this enterprise is indicative of his ability to move quickly to put deals together, outfox his competitors, and convince others to follow his lead. He has invested $20 million of his own money in Pershing Gold.

Additionally, over the past 24 months, Barry has purchased 10 million shares in the open market. The story of Pershing Gold begins in 2009 when Barry took a company public through a reverse merger, raising $4 million. He also took a seat on the board. But as all the Superstars will tell you, not every deal works out as planned. The business model was flawed and the management team did not execute. "When the CEO and CFO burned through all the cash, I had to figure out a way to create value for my friends who helped fund the company," he says. "So I bought two pieces of dirt in Nevada for $2 million. I then found an asset that I could purchase out of bankruptcy, a fully permitted mine, for $20 million. However, I had four weeks to find the money to complete the acquisition. I gave them a $2 million deposit and a Letter of Intent." (See Figure 10.4.)

Turning the proverbial lemon into lemonade, he put together a deal to acquire a uranium company for which he had just raised $20 million.

"I was lucky, as the Fukushima meltdown happened about the time I was working on the Nevada transaction. Uranium companies blew up. I had

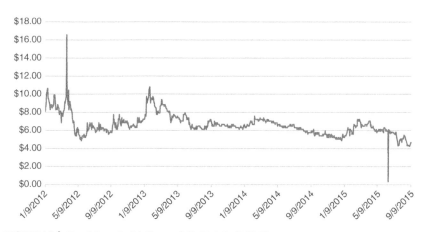

FIGURE 10.4 Pershing Gold Corp. (NASDAQ: PGLC)
Data Source: Thomson Reuters Corporation.

helped raise money for the uranium company as well, so now I had two companies that I had put friends in that were not working. Now I had two companies to save. My reputation was on the line."

He issued stock in the newly formed gold company, the "two pieces of dirt" in Nevada, and Pershing Gold acquired the uranium company, American Energy Fuels, taking $18 million of the cash in the uranium play to finalize the purchase of the asset of the Relief Canyon properties in Nevada. Pershing Gold later spun out the uranium assets. His next step was to find a superstar CEO to build Pershing Gold.

"I knew nothing about gold except the gold I got my wife at the jewelry store," he explains.

"I needed management, so I called Pierre Lassonde, the president of Franco-Nevada (NYSE: FNV), who is one of the most famous people in the gold business, and I asked him how I should go about finding a top-notch CEO for Pershing Gold. He basically said I should either try to recruit the best people from the best companies or use a headhunter."

Barry called Franco-Nevada's head of North American Operations, Steve Alfers, offered him $500,000 in cash and 10% of Pershing Gold to take over the CEO position. Alfers accepted the offer in September 2011 and has quietly been building the company, preparing it for a listing on the NYSE. The company is expected to go into production sometime in 2015.

As for Barry, he is adamant. "My biggest deal right now is Pershing Gold. It's going to be a $1 billion market cap company. This is my biggest deal ever."

As the Company literature states, Pershing Gold has consolidated a 39-square-mile land package in mining-friendly Lovelock, Nevada, neighboring significant current and past producing mines. Nearby producing mines include Coeur d'Alene's (NYSE: CDE) bordering Rochester mine, which has been producing for 30 years.

Coeur d'Alene, the largest U.S.-based silver producer, with a market cap of $725 million, has a current strategic investment in Pershing Gold. Under Steve Alfers' leadership, Pershing Gold has more than tripled its gold resource to a measured and indicated 552,000 ounces.

H.C. Wainwright recently issued a "Buy" rating on Pershing Gold and 12-month target price of $0.70.

"Not only do I look after myself, but it is very important to me to stay with the company until it works. I have been in this business for over 10 years because I look out for my investors. If I put my money into the stock, and that of friends and family, I owe it to them to do everything I can to make the company successful," says Honig.

If you are going to invest in the microcap space, get in early, and sometimes you want to get out early, because most small-cap companies will have to keep raising money. If they are successful, they will keep raising money to grow; if they are not successful, they will need to raise money to stay alive. Invest alongside guys who have been in the game, and get in as early as possible.

Barry, like most of the Superstars, has more than once sold his position too early and left money on the table. The microcap space is like a perpetual game of poker. The lyrics in the song, "The Gambler," made famous by Kenny Rogers, though clichéd, sums up the quandary in which microcap investors often find themselves: "You got to know when to hold 'em, know when to fold 'em, know when to walk away, know when to run."

Honig's experience has taught him that "the biggest score is not necessarily the biggest win; it's about the big win in the shortest period of time. Sometimes I have gotten out too early. I could have made 5 or 10 times more; I have been too smart for my own good, but other times I have anticipated potential pitfalls before other investors saw them, and been right to get out when I did." I asked him to give me an example of a situation where he got out too early. "Akeena Solar did a reverse merge at a $10 million market cap in 2007. Not too long after they went public, they needed a second round of financing, and they couldn't raise money, so I funded it. The stock went to $17, but I sold my stock at $5, and though I made $7 million, I did well, I could have made a lot more, but I got out early because I didn't think the margins were good enough, and additionally they had no proprietary technology.

"You know people complain that I buy cheap stock," he says. "You're damn right I do. I'm the early investor in most of these deals. I'm fixing them or helping create them."

Though he currently has positions in approximately 50 stocks, most of whom he has helped raise capital for, consulted with, or restructured, Barry is always on the hunt for new opportunities. He is presented with as many as 10 new opportunities per week, he says. One he is particularly excited about is RantMedia, still private as of the writing of this chapter. He has invested several million dollars of his own money and raised $10 million for them.

RantMedia

RantMedia is a Los Angeles–based company, founded by a college baseball player in 2010. They started with two full-time employees and 50 paid sports bloggers. By the end of 2012, they had grown the company to seven employees and 250 contract writers, reaching 4.7 million monthly unique visitors and 55 million monthly page views. In November 2013, Barry raised $3 million for RantMedia. They are now ranked by comScore as the second largest independent sports website in the United States and the eleventh largest sports website overall in the United States. The company is profitable with triple-digit annual revenue growth. With the launch of RantLifestyle, RantChic, and RantGirls, they now reach 27 million unique visitors monthly. Honig's expectation is the company will be bought out in the near term.

VBI Vaccines (NASDAQ: VBIV)

VBI went public in July 2014 on the NASDAQ (Figure 10.5). The chairman, Dr. Steven Gillis, PhD, is an immunologist by training with expertise in molecular and tumor immunology. He is a rock star in the world of biotechs. He was the founder and CEO of Corixa, which was acquired in 2005 by GSK for $300 million. Prior to Corixa, Dr. Gillis was founder and director of Immunex, acquired in 2002 by Amgen for $16 billion.

As a private company, VBI raised $49 million. Investors included Clarus Ventures, ARCH Venture Partners, and 5AM Ventures. The company has developed eVLPs, a third-generation class of synthetic vaccines that closely resemble the structure of the virus they mimic. They are suitable to a wide array of viruses, including CMV, HCV, Dengue, RSV, and West Nile, and have demonstrated an ability to trigger strong, broadly neutralizing antibodies in multiple preclinical models.

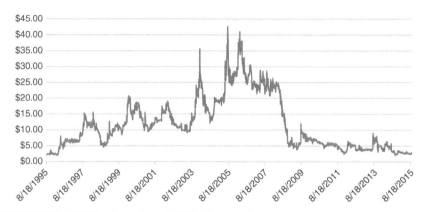

FIGURE 10.5 VBI Vaccines, Inc. (NASDAQ: VBIV)
Data Source: Thomson Reuters Corporation.

Drone Aviation (OTCQB: DRNE)

Drone Aviation Holding Corp. provides aerial- and land-based surveillance and communications solutions to government and commercial customers. Utilizing a unique tethering capability, the company operates in the National Airspace within Federal Aviation Administration (FAA) guidelines for the drone market and provides distinct advantages, including mobility and substantially reduced acquisition and operating costs. These product characteristics have enabled DRNE to establish sales with various divisions of the U.S. Department of Defense, NASA, BLM, the Department of Agriculture, several state DOT and municipal agencies, universities, and various Fortune 500 companies.

> His return on equity is extraordinary by any measure. He is up by 6:30 a.m., in the office by 8 a.m., sitting at his desk with four screens and a Bloomberg terminal. Part of his day he is trading while simultaneously working on his deals and evaluating companies for financing. His pace is frenetic, but disciplined. He does not have long phone conversations. I have never seen him on a call for more than two minutes. He is a paragon of efficiency.

In my estimation, Honig runs the most efficient operation in the microcap sector. He has a staff of four: two MBAs, his brother, and an executive assistant.

When one does a deal with Honig, he will get less, but doing a deal with him often means less is more. He brings a network of professional investors, businessmen, marketers, bloggers, analysts, newsletter writers, and his own deep pockets into the deal. Not every deal he has been involved in has worked out for investors. He has been a clock builder and a time teller, a builder of companies and a trader.

Barry Honig Top Stock Positions

Barry Honig

Company	Ticker	Position (m)	Mkt Value ($m)
Pershing Gold Corp.	PGLC.PK	4.10	17.83
ChromaDex Corp.	CDXC.PK	8.41	10.10
Marathon Patent Group Inc.	MARA.O	0.66	5.55
MusclePharm Corp.	MSLP.PK	0.33	3.86
VBI Vaccines Inc.	VBIV.O	0.99	3.23
Cocrystal Pharma Inc.	COCP.OB	1.43	0.60
Ruthigen Inc.	RTGN.O	0.04	0.41
Inventergy Global Inc.	INVT.O	2.92	0.91
USell.com Inc.	USEL.PK	0.76	0.86
Sevion Therapeutics Inc.	SVON.OB	1.24	1.28
Orbital Tracking Corp	TRKK.OB	0.07	0.06
Passport Potash Inc.	PPI.V	7.64	0.13
Bullfrog Gold Corp.	BFGC.PK	2.87	0.07
WPCS International Inc.	WPCS.O	0.15	0.23

*.O, .OQ, TQ means NASDAQ and .K NYSE.
Source: Thomson Reuters Corporation.

Note

1. Amir Efrati, "Yahoo Buys Interclick for $270 Million," *Wall Street Journal,* November 1, 2011.

CHAPTER 11

Manny Villafana

The hardest part of raising capital for CPI was that we were totally unknown. I was a young Puerto Rican living in Minneapolis, a land of Midwesterners. I had no previous history in manufacturing or inventing anything. Imagine you go to an investor and say, "We're going to make a better pacemaker," and they say, "Doesn't Medtronic make a pacemaker?"

—Manny Villafana, CEO, Kips Bay Medical

Occupation: CEO, Kips Bay Medical (NASDAQ: KIPS)

Age: 76

Education: High school degree, Cardinal Hayes

Estimated Net Worth: $25 million

Status: Married, five children

Residence: Minneapolis, MN

Favorite Stock: Kips Bay Medical (NASDAQ: KIPS)

Advice: "You've got to make a decision to devote a decade of your life; it takes ten years of your life to accomplish anything."

Greatest Book Ever Read: *Undaunted Courage,* Stephen Ambrose

Hobbies: Reading history

Heroes: Wright Brothers, Lewis and Clark

Born into a poor family from Puerto Rico, Manny Villafana grew up in the Bronx. Though he never earned a college degree, he founded two of the biggest medical device companies in the world. He owes much of his childhood stability to a boys' club called Kips Bay, which he joined in 1949 when he was 10 years old. The club gave him a job, leadership opportunities, and a place to hang out.

He worked the cloakroom at the club for 40 cents an hour every day after school and also did odd jobs for the club, which included working in the clinic, assisting in such things as weighing the kids and writing notes to the parents. Through his work at the club, Villafana learned the importance of frugality, industry, and hard work.

There Is Something of the Horatio Alger Story in Villafana's Life

"We had nothing, zero, *nada*," he says. "My parents were immigrants from Puerto Rico, my father could not write his name. He wrote with the proverbial *X*, and my mother only had a third-grade education. My father died when I was 10 years old."

His boyhood days were disciplined. Though he lost his father when he was young, Manny stayed on the straight-and-narrow path. Most of the money he made at the club he gave to his mother to help run the household, and as he got older he paid his own tuition to attend Cardinal Hayes, a prominent all-boys Catholic high school founded in 1941. Though they offered him a scholarship based on need, he turned them down. Instead, he used wages earned at the boys' club to pay the $10-a-month tuition. He developed, as he puts it, an affinity for math and science. At age 17, he graduated from Cardinal Hayes. Interestingly, Regis Philbin, Martin Scorsese, and John Sweeney, president of the AFL-CIO, 1995–2009, also graduated from Cardinal Hayes. After graduating, Manny briefly attended Manhattan College, but soon dropped out as he could not afford the tuition.

One of the benefits of working at the Kips Bay Boys Club was that Manny met a lot of interesting people. In 1957, through his connections at the club, he got a job at Engineering Laboratories, a company founded in the 1920s in Yonkers, New York. The company initially made amateur radio equipment, but later the business evolved into making and selling highly sophisticated electronic communications equipment for the military. His first job there was in the print shop learning how to print documents and collating manuals that went with the equipment they manufactured. Within a year, he was promoted to the engineering department where he worked as an aid to the engineers. "I picked up a lot of electronics in my four years at the company," he says.

His next job was at the Ethyl Corporation, which was founded in 1922 as a "joint venture between General Motors, DuPont, and Standard Oil of New Jersey (Exxon)."

Ethyl Corporation was a chemical additives company famous for its "anti-knock" chemical additive for gasoline. Today, the company is part of

NewMarket Corporation, a multinational concern operating in the petroleum additives industry.[1]

He worked as an assistant to the business manager and learned technical writing and drawing. Part of his job entailed getting gasoline samples from various gas stations, testing the octane levels of the gasoline to see how good or bad it was, and then publishing a report that was sent to the gasoline manufacturers. After reading the reports, the gasoline manufacturers would buy Ethyl's tetraethyl lead, a chemical additive for gasoline that reduced the knocking sound in gasoline-powered engines and "prevented exhaust valve and seat wear."

"I enhanced my chemistry background," he says, "which would prove helpful in my later endeavors."

Next up for Villafana was Picker X-Ray, at the time one of the world's three largest X-ray manufacturers along with Westinghouse and General Electric. The company was a leader in the field of advanced cobalt therapy for cancer and a major designer and supplier of operating room X-ray machines.[2]

At Picker X-Ray, Villafana fortuitously was chosen to do technical sales and became the middleman between representatives of Picker X-Ray in Europe, Asia, and South America and the suppliers of parts for cardiovascular heart devices. One of those devices was the pacemaker.

After working at Picker for three years, he was hired by Medtronic (NYSE: MDT) in 1967. Earl Pakkan, then the CEO of Medtronic, hired Villafana to help set up a new international division in Paris as they were expanding operations in Europe, setting up their own factories to manufacture parts they were previously buying from middlemen. With the expansion of their European operations, they were able to cut costs.

Founded in 1949 by a graduate student in electrical engineering from the University of Minnesota and his brother in law, Medtronic began as a repair shop fixing medical devices for the University of Minnesota research labs.[3] The Medtronic story is a fascinating study in how big companies start small. By the 1950s the company was "designing and producing new devices needed for research" primarily for medical equipment manufacturers and research labs. Their "first life-changing therapy, a wearable, battery-powered cardiac pacemaker, was the foundation for many more Medtronic therapies that used [its] electrical stimulation expertise to improve the lives of millions of people."[4]

While other companies had invented pacemakers, until Medtronic's pacemaker, "they were bulky, relied on external electrodes, and had to be plugged into a wall outlet. These AC-operated pacemakers could fail during a power blackout." By the end of the 1960s, Medtronic had developed an implantable pacemaker that sold for $375. By 1968, revenue had grown to $12 million and net income to $1 million.[5] Medtronic's 2014 revenue was $17 billion. Big companies start small.

Villafana worked for Medtronic from 1967 to 1972, steadily gaining knowledge and building a network of professionals in the medical device industry that he would leverage when he started his first company in February 1972, Cardiac Pacemakers Inc. (CPI).

Villafana started CPI with $50,000 after watching a demonstration by the inventor of a new lithium battery that could be used in pacemakers, a technology that would dramatically increase the longevity of the product.

☆ ☆ ☆

Medtronic was a high-flying company, and we were going against them. Investors said, 'If it was such a great idea, Medtronic would have done it.' To make matters worse, Medtronic was suing my company. The fact is Medtronic rejected it. The inventor of the new power source came to Medtronic and they said it couldn't work. They said no, we don't want it. The developer of the new power source then came to me, and I said, 'Let's do it.'"

Medtronic and other manufacturers were for the most part still using a technology based on the mercury battery.

In 1971, the lithium-iodide cell, invented by Wilson Greatbatch, an American inventor who held over 350 patents, was ready for commercialization.

The fact that the best and brightest scientists behind the research and development of pacemakers did not react positively to the new technology created an opportunity for Villafana, and he wasted no time capitalizing on it. He saw what the "experts" missed. I am reminded here of Paul Johnson's book, *Intellectuals*, a study of the decisions of "great thinkers" who consistently got it wrong on the big issues of their day.

I am also reminded of Roger Lowenstein's book, *Origins of the Crash*, a look at the 1990s Internet boom and bust. He shows empirically that analysts during that period consistently got it wrong on the Internet companies they covered, putting "Buy" ratings on companies that were fundamentally flawed.

There are two important business lessons here: One, if something sounds too good to be true, it may be, but take a hard, close look before rejecting it. Two, the experts, the analysts, and the media pundits are wrong as often as they are right. Today, pacemakers still use lithium as their power source.

On February 2, 1972, CPI opened its doors. Three months later it went public as a pink-sheet, over-the-counter stock, raising $450,000, on May 26, 1972. The company later listed on the NASDAQ. The IPO was led by investment bank Craig-Hallum, from Minneapolis, Minnesota, where the company was based.

Within six years, CPI grew revenue to $46 million by selling a better, longer lasting pacemaker than the competition. "Theirs lasted 18 months, ours lasted 18 to 30 years," explains Villafana.

Remarkably, CPI implanted its first pacemaker on November 29, 1972, just nine months after opening its doors. "Back then the FDA did not take charge of medical device products. It was a lot easier to get things done, to get products to market. It wasn't until May 28, 1976, that the FDA was given the right to regulate medical devices," Manny explains. For a short period of time, Villafana notes, CPI had exclusive rights to the new lithium battery.

Thus, CPI had no regulatory issues to deal with during the first four years of its existence. Sales of their longer lasting pacemaker exploded. In 1976, Manny left CPI. Two years later, when CPI was purchased by Eli Lilly for $127 million, he became a multimillionaire at the age of 39. Later, Eli Lilly would refocus its business on biopharma products and spin CPI out as a separate entity called Guidant.

In 2006, Guidant was purchased by Boston Scientific for $27.2 billion, outbidding Johnson & Johnson in a deal that was highly criticized by Wall Street. Boston Scientific and Guidant were having quality related problems with many of their products at the time, including the newly acquired pacemaker technology. Boston Scientific's stock would plummet from $35 in 2006 to just $7.00 a couple of years later as they fell deeply into debt and sales stagnated.

Manny sold all but 2% of his stock in the Eli Lilly buyout in 1978. But by that time he was already on to his next venture.

Again, he would use his keen judgment, analytical skills, and his capacity for risk to start his next company in 1976. St. Jude Medical (Figure 11.1) was based on the idea that the world needed a better heart valve. As Villafana explains it, he met some doctors from Beth Israel Hospital who told him that their patients had a lot of problems with the heart valves they were implanting. Thus was born his idea for a new heart valve. Just two years after going public, St. Jude entered the market with a "bi-leaflet implantable heart value."

The purpose of artificial heart valves is to "maintain unimpeded forward flow through the heart and from the heart into the major blood vessels connected to the heart, the pulmonary artery and the aorta." Human hearts contain four valves. When they malfunction, it can result in heart failure. The St. Jude valve eliminated much of the issues with earlier heart valve technology, such as the body's low tolerance for the devices and their propensity to create backflow. St Jude, he notes, was one of the first companies to go through the FDA approval process for a medical device.

The St. Jude Medical "innovative heart valve design became the gold standard for mechanical heart valves" in the 1980s.[6] In fact, the St. Jude heart valve is still used more than any heart valve in the world. Villafana stayed

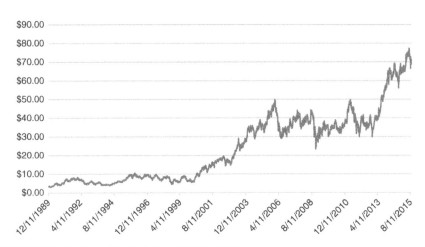

FIGURE 11.1 St. Jude Medical Inc. (NYSE: STJ)
Data Source: Thomson Reuters Corporation.

with the company until 1982. That same year, he founded GV Medical, a company that "developed a device to open blood vessels."

Five years later, he founded ATS Medical, where his team developed a bi-leaflet valve "that uses an open-pivot design to reduce clots and improve blood flow."

In 2000, he raised $10 million and launched CABG Medical, where for six years his team tried to develop an artificial artery for coronary bypass surgery. The company was not successful and closed in 2006. When asked why the artificial graft did not work, he said, "We tested it in pigs. It worked great. Our mistake was that we didn't realize that because pigs have four legs the way the graft was positioned in their bodies made the flow of blood work beautifully, no kinking, no problems. Humans have two legs and walk upright, an obviously different anatomical structure. The graft simply did not work. It kinked, it leaked. It could not maintain the flow of blood properly."

Not to be discouraged, in 2008 he founded Kips Bay Medical (NASDAQ: KIPS; see Figure 11.2), named after the boys' club where he spent much of his youth. The technology (eSVS Mesh) his team is developing was acquired from Medtronic in 2007. It is a wire mesh that envelopes or functions as a sleeve for saphenous vein grafts during coronary artery bypass surgery, "preventing the damaging expansion of the vein graft," which the company hopes will reduce or prevent resulting injury, which "can lead to saphenous vein graft failure."[7]

On February 10, 2014, Kips Bay Medical announced their first Austrian implant of the eSVS Mesh. The implant was done at the Medical University of Vienna, the largest medical training facility in the German-speaking region, according to the press release.

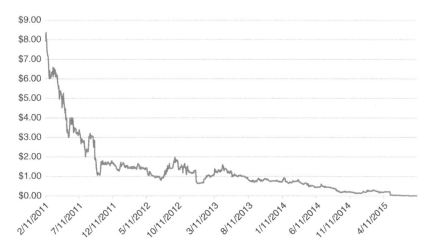

FIGURE 11.2 Kips Bay Medical Inc. (OTC: KIPS)
Data Source: Thomson Reuters Corporation.

Unfortunately, the clinical trials did not go well. Over three years they enrolled 106 patients, but when the eSVS Mesh failed on seven of the first ten patients after 6 months, the company canceled the trial and moved to liquidate the company. Again, not every idea works. What looks promising today may be a grand failure tomorrow. Small stocks can also lead to big losses. The stock is trading at .01 cent, market cap $432,000 (September 4, 2015).

Manny Villafana enjoys reading American history. He loves reading about the men and women who developed our country, men and women who had the biggest challenges of all. "The greatest book I ever read was *Undaunted Courage*, by Stephen Ambrose.[8] The book is about Meriwether Lewis and the Lewis and Clark Expedition commissioned by Thomas Jefferson in 1803. When Thomas Jefferson told Lewis and Clark, I want you to go across the country in a boat, against the Indians, the cold, the unknown, and chart it out for us, they could have refused, but they took up the challenge. We can learn from them about what it means to take risks, to forge ahead when you don't have the answers, when you're moving into the great unknown."

Villafana is also inspired by the Wright Brothers. "Two weeks before they put a plane in the air, the *New York Times* said, 'We won't have an aircraft that works for 1,000 years,'" he explains.

"In 1899, Dr. Duell, head of the U.S. patent office, said, 'Everything that can be invented has been invented.' And now the experts say, 'We've been doing coronary bypass surgery the way we do it now for the past 50 years and Kips Bay Medical is going to change that? I doubt it.' My job is to prove them wrong."

Manny Villafana's accomplishments are of historical significance. Consider the fact that he started two companies that would become two of the biggest medical device companies in the history of the world, Cardiac Pacemakers, which would ultimately become Guidant Corporation, valued at $27.2 billion in 2006, and St. Jude Medical, which today is a Fortune 500 company with sales of $5.5 billion.

> It is remarkable that a man with only a high school education rose up out of the ghettos of the Bronx, and with no formal scientific training, founded two companies that became the biggest in their industries. His work will reverberate through the annals of medical history. Whether the technology of Kips Bay Medical fails or succeeds, Manny Villafana has made his mark on history. He is a Superstar.

Words of Wisdom from Manny Villafana

1. "You've got to make a decision to devote a decade of your life to something. It takes 10 years of your life to accomplish anything."
2. "You must believe you're better than the average guy; it's hard, difficult, you cry at night."
3. "It's harder and always takes longer than you anticipate."
4. "A lot of critics said, 'You can't do it, Manny, you can't do it.' It's much more difficult on the medical side because of the regulations."
5. "With life-and-death products, if we're wrong, you have a dead patient on the table."
6. "Doctors say, 'You want me to put that in a human body; if it doesn't work, the patient is dead, I'm dead, you're dead.'"

Manny Villafana's List of Achievements and Awards

- Minnesota Science and Technology Hall of Fame
- Recipient of the Ellis Island Medal of Honor
- Living Legend of Medicine Award from the World Society of Cardiothoracic Surgeons
- Minnesota Business Hall of Fame
- Grand Prize Recipient, Mediterranean Institute of Cardiology
- Boys and Girls Club of America Hall of Fame
- National Entrepreneur of the Year Award in the Master category

Manny Villafana Top Stock Positions

Manny Villafana

Company	Ticker	Position (m)	Market Value ($m)
Kips Bay Medical Inc.	NASDAQ: KIPS	6.89	0.11

Source: Thomson Reuters Corporation.

Notes

1. NewMarket Corporation, "Our History," www.newmarket.com/About/Pages/OurHistory.aspx.
2. "Harvey Picker, 92, Pioneer in Patient-Centered Care, Is Dead," *New York Times*, March 29, 2008.
3. Medtronic, "Our Story: The Garage Years," www.medtronic.eu/about-medtronic/our-story/garage-years/index.htm.
4. Medtronic, "Company Profile," www.medtronic.com/2011Citizenship Update/corporate-citizenship/company-profile.html.
5. Medtronic, "Our Story," http://adriatic.medtronic.com/about-medtronic/our-story/index.htm.
6. St. Jude Medical, "A History of Innovation for Comprehensive Solutions," sjm.com/corporate/about-us/history.
7. Kips Bay Medical Company Profile, 2014.
8. Stephen E. Ambrose, *Undaunted Courage: Meriwether Lewis, Thomas Jefferson, and the Opening of the American West* (New York: Touchstone, 1996).

CHAPTER 12

Buzz Heidkte

Be patient when buying. It might take six months to accumulate a position; you should be in for the long term and remember 20% of microcaps go to zero.

—Buzz Heidkte, Owner, MidSouth Investor Fund

Occupation: Owner, MidSouth Investor Fund, Family Office

Age: 73

Education: BSc in Business, Tennessee Tech

Estimated Net Worth: $20 million

Residence: Nashville, TN

Nickname: "Buzz"

Best Stock Picks of his Career: Pre-Paid Legal, Patrick Industries (NAS-DAQ: PATK), Books-A-Million (NASDAQ: BAMM)

Investment Advice: "Don't put too much money in any one stock; spread it out; you never know which ones will be your big winner."

Favorite Books: None, but reads 45 publications and newspapers. Buzz is a weekly contributor to the *RedChip Money Report* weekly newsletter.

Hobbies: Travel, tennis, fine restaurants

The son of a military man, Buzz Heidkte grew up in Nashville, Tennessee. He began his career in the financial markets at the tail end of Wall Street's "go-go" years in 1968. In late June 1962, the Dow stood at 535.76, but by the time Buzz was in his junior year at Tennessee Tech in 1966, the Dow had reached a then all-time-high of 995.15. Timothy Leary, Ken Kesey, and Jack Kerouac were not the only ones reaching new highs in the sixties.

One newsletter writer during the sixties put it this way: "For some time there has been a suspicion on Wall Street that the stock market and the hemlines of women's skirts move in the same direction." Low interest rates, the growth of mutual funds, conglomerates, and the rise of tech stocks such as Polaroid, Telex, Texas Instruments, Itek, and Xerox were some of the defining characteristics of the go-go years.

John Brooks wrote the seminal work about the era, titled: *The Go-Go Years: The Drama and Crashing Finale of Wall Street's Bullish 60s*.[1]

Influenced by his dad, who was an engineer and accountant who dabbled in the stock market, Buzz was an early convert to the financial markets. He began reading the *Wall Street Journal* in eighth grade. In fact, he tried to get a job at a brokerage firm when he was only 16 years old. After graduating from Tennessee Tech with a degree in Business in 1967, he traveled to three southern cities, Nashville, Memphis, and Atlanta, trying to get a job at one of the white-shoe firms—Goldman Sachs, Merrill Lynch, Lehman Brothers—but according to Buzz, "They would hire only blue-bloods back then."

He did land a job at an insurance company as a systems analyst, a "plum" job as he called it, but he quickly became tired of it and landed his first Wall Street job a year later with Dominick and Dominick, a firm that had been around since the 1860s. In 1968, he took a job as a stock broker with Spencer Trask, an institutional trading firm. Several years later he moved to a firm called Thomson McKinnon, a New York Investment Bank, where he polished his skills. Fifteen years later, at the age of 37, he started a limited real estate partnership in Nashville that also dabbled in the stock market.

In 1985, he began writing a newsletter to Tennessee investors covering local public companies. Within a few years, he built a subscriber base of 2,000 high-net-worth investors. By 1986, his firm had evolved into a full-service broker-dealer, making markets and writing research, with both retail and institutional trading desks.

In 1993, he complemented the broker-dealer with a hedge fund, Mid-South Partners, focusing primarily on microcap stocks. He notes that the fund's best year ever was in 2009, when it returned 74%. He had positioned in smaller stocks that were battered in the great recession of 2007–2008 and reaped the rewards in 2009. When evaluating opportunities in the market, he looks for the following:

- Stocks with a price-to-earnings ratio under 10
- Stocks trading under book value
- Stocks trading under 25% of sales per share
- Stocks trading under 5× cash flow
- Stocks with sales growth of 20% or more over the previous quarter

One of the fund's best picks was Pre-Paid Legal. "In the late '90s," he explains, "I had the CEO in my office. The stock was trading at 1 5/8 at the time. He told me that one of their problems was they had to pay sales people too much. He said to correct the problem, they were going to spread commissions over a period of years. Well, they corrected the problem. I got out of the stock at $35.00 in 2002."

A brief history of Pre-Paid Legal reinforces one of the themes of this book: Big companies start small. Pre-Paid Legal was founded in 1972 by an insurance salesman, who after a car accident realized that his legal fees were not covered by his insurance. In a meeting with Buzz in the late 1990s, the founder and CEO, Harland C. Stonecipher, the son of a sharecropper, shared his story with him.

If I hadn't had the accident, I probably would have started a life insurance company. If you wait until you know all the answers, you're not going to start. My theory is simple: Ready, fire, aim. I think that's the story of anybody who makes a success. What that means is that you adjust your course as you go along. Looking back, it seems like everything I've done was like jumping off a cliff. But it seems like when I've jumped, things have come out fairly well.[2]

Pre-Paid Legal revenue grew from $4.2 million in 1983 to $42 million in 1986. In 1997, the company generated $60 million in revenue.

In 2010, revenue for Pre-Paid Legal reached $454 million and $67 million in net income (Figure 12.1). On January 31, 2011, Pre-Paid Legal announced that Miocene Partners, a private equity firm in New York, would purchase the company for $650 million, $66.50 a share, a 10% premium to the closing price of the stock on January 28.[3] Stonecipher made about $60 million on the deal.

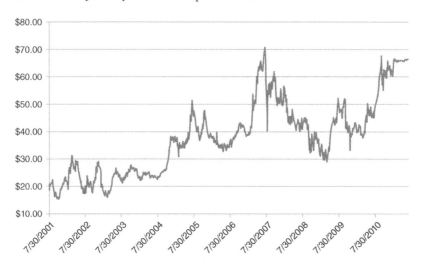

FIGURE 12.1 **Pre-Paid Legal Services (NYSE: PPD)**
Data Source: Thomson Reuters Corporation.

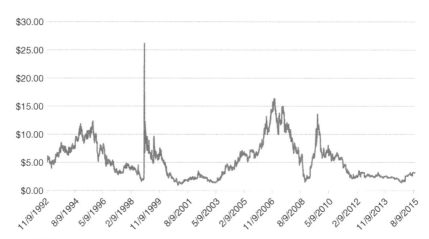

FIGURE 12.2 Books-A-Million (NASDAQ: BAMM)
Data Source: Thomson Reuters Corporation.

One of the keys to Heidkte's success is that he tries to "buy the right stocks for the right time. When you get older and wiser you understand this better. After 9/11, I started positioning in Books-A-Million (Figure 12.2), as I figured people would be sitting home more reading books. The stock doubled in a year," he says.

Buzz is a speed reader. Though he doesn't read a lot of books, he does read about 45 different publications, he says. "I'm looking for trends, ideas on where the world is heading." He names a few of the publications he reads: *Vanity Fair, National Enquirer, Town and Country, Forbes, Fortune, Information Week, New York Times, Investors Business Daily,* and the local papers. And he adds, "I love to read financial statements." During my interview, he quips: "I was reading today that the number of houses in the market for sale is the lowest in 13 years. I did some homework and decided to buy Patrick Industries (NASDAQ: PATK). I saw insider buying by the CFO, low multiples, only 6× earnings. They are in the manufactured housing business."

At the time of this interview, July 2013, the stock was trading around $22–$23.00. On September 9, 2014, the stock closed at $42.09 with a 52-week high of $49.10 (Figure 12.3). One year later, September 2015, the stock has a $692 million market cap and is trading at $44.00. With the revolution in natural gas exploration and discoveries, he is currently focused on companies operating in the natural gas industry.

Biggest Mistake
"Investing in China stocks listed in the United States. I couldn't get over how much fraud there was over there."

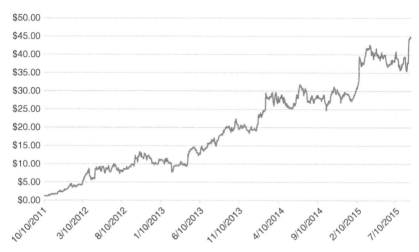

FIGURE 12.3 Patrick Industries (NASDAQ: PATK)
Data Source: Thomson Reuters Corporation.

Most Important Lessons Learned in Microcaps

- "Stay away from story stocks; if you buy 100 of those things, you will end up losing a lot of money."
- "Be patient when buying. It might take six months to accumulate a position; you should be in for the long term and remember 20% of microcaps go to zero."
- "I am looking for those with the potential for 100% gains and greater to offset those that go to zero, but I only buy those that have earnings."
- "Look at what you can afford to lose; it's a numbers game."
- "Don't put too much money in any one stock; spread it out; you never know which ones will be your big winner."

Notes

1. John Brooks, *The Go-Go Years: The Drama and Crashing Finale of Wall Street's Bullish 60s* (New York: John Wiley & Sons, 1973).
2. Jay P. Pederson, *International Directory of Company Histories*, vol. 20 (Boston: St. James Press, 1998).
3. Dealbook, "Pre-Paid Legal in $650 Million Buyout," *New York Times*, January 31, 2011.

CHAPTER 13

Greg Sichenzia

Microcaps are a three-card-monte play. If you don't know how to play, stay away.

—Greg Sichenzia, Sichenzia Ross Friedman Ference LLP

Occupation: Founding Partner, Sichenzia Ross Friedman Ference LLP

Age: 54

Education: BS in Political Science and Economics, American University; JD, Benjamin N. Cardozo School of Law

Estimated Net Worth: $25 million

Nickname: "The Warrior"

Marital Status: Married, three children

Hobbies: Reading, traveling to exotic places

Favorite Financial Books: *The Scorpion and the Frog*, Salvatore Lauria as told to David S. Barry

If you are a CEO, hedge fund, institution, or investment banker working in the microcap world, it is important to have a knowledgeable and well-respected law firm. One of the top firms in the space is Sichenzia Ross Friedman Ference LLP, founded by Gregory Sichenzia in 1998. Gregory Sichenzia is a talker and joker, a charismatic personality, and according to his associates, he is a "warrior." He is also a hard worker, smart, savvy, and disciplined. He arrives at the office by 8 a.m. and rarely leaves before 7 p.m. "If I'm not knee-deep in business at all times, I am not happy," he explains. His creativity, innovation, and entrepreneurial spirit have enabled him to build one of the most successful law firms in the country servicing small public companies.

Unlike most of the Superstars in this book, he cannot recall any significant influencer in his life. His parents divorced when he was young. He makes it clear during the interview that he did not live a privileged life. "My dad did not give me a dime. I worked in a supermarket as a kid, collecting carts in parking lots and stocking shelves for $2.60 an hour."

He studied political science and economics at American University, a prelude to his law degree, which he earned in 1987 from the Benjamin N. Cardoza School of Law. While in college at American University in Washington, D.C., he worked at the Kennedy Center selling candy during the intermissions of concerts and plays.

He began his career at Finley Krumble, a white-shoe firm serving mostly larger-cap public companies. He then moved to smaller law firms and in 1998, at the age of 36, he started his own firm with two partners, renting six offices in Manhattan. Today his firm has over 50 lawyers with hundreds of clients. His firm has handled the legal work for thousands of transactions. "I decided early on to specialize in SEC law as it relates to microcaps. We are one of the few firms on Wall Street that operate specifically in this area," he says.

His law firm initially built its business and reputation representing small-cap IPOs. In 1999, when the IPO market fell, Sichenzia's firm began advising PIPE transactions (private investment in public entities).

Not only does Sichenzia's firm conduct the IPO and PIPE preparatory work, writing prospectuses, filing registration statements, and representing issuers post-IPO, the firm also, through its vast network of hedge funds, family offices, and broker-dealers, provides capital raising consultation as well with a particular focus on public companies raising $10 million to $20 million. His firm has consistently ranked number one in PIPE transactions.

One of the important keys to his firm's success is that its attorneys are accessible to its clients. They were one of the first to move to a fixed fee paradigm, and one of the first firms to focus exclusively on small companies, which has grown to representing many large-cap companies as well. Given his wide ranging experience in the microcap space, investors would be wise to consider his advice:

Gregory Sichenzia's Advice to Microcap Investors
1. "There are lots of players looming in the shadows to hurt small public companies. You have to learn how to separate the good from the bad. It's easier to perpetrate fraud in the microcap sector than it is for the bigger companies. Watch out for shell promoters and nominee accounts among those who own stocks in shells."
2. "Get to know the management teams of these companies and the people who own the shells they reverse into. The guys holding the stock in the reverse merger deals are the guys getting rich."

3. "Be cognizant of what accounting firms and law firms the companies are using."
4. "There can be tremendous awards in this space, but you must be careful."
5. "A lot of people in the microcap space play on the fringes."
6. "Microcaps are not for the casual investor."
7. "If you don't know your way around, you can get slaughtered."
8. "Microcaps are a three-card-monte play. If you don't know how to play, stay away."
9. "There are exceptions and dumb luck, but you have to be savvy in this space."

Stock List

List of Stocks Mentioned in This Book

Company	Ticker	Industry	Market Cap
Actinium Pharma, Inc.	NYSE: ATNM	Biotechnology	100.37M
American Caresource Holdings Inc.	NASDAQCM: ANCI	Specialized Health Services	8.16M
Arc Equities	Private	Specialty Finance	–
Apple Inc.	NASDAQGS: AAPL	Electronic Equipment	640.47 B
Aurora Toys	Bought by Nabisco	Toys	–
Big North Graphite Corp.	OTC PINK: BNCIF	Graphite	0.35M
Blockbuster	Private	Home Entertainment	–
Books-A-Million Inc.	NASDAQGS: BAMM	Specialty Retail	49.31M
Boston Scientific Corp.	NYSE: BSX	Medical Appliances & Equipment	22.78B
Cancer Genetics Inc.	NASDAQCM: CGIX	Medical Laboratories & Research	100.67M
Cantel Medical Corp.	NYSE: CMN	Medical Instruments & Supplies	2.08B
Cardiac Pacemakers	Bought out by Eli Lilly	Medical Devices	–
Careguide Inc.	OTC: CGUE	Commercial Services	–
Caremark	Bought out by CVS	Home Healthcare	–
China Power Equipment Inc.	OTC PINK: CPQQ	Electrical Equipment	705.71K
ChromaDex Corp.	OTCQB: CDXC	Chemicals, Major Diversified	147.74M
CNS Response Inc.	OTCQB: CNSO	Diagnostic Substances	4.88M
Coeur Mining Inc.	NYSE: CDE	Silver	415.46M
ConMed Healthcare Management Inc.	NASDAQGS: CNMD	Medical Appliances & Equipment	1.44B

(Continued)

Company	Ticker	Industry	Market Cap
Franco-Nevada Corp.	NYSE: FNV	Gold	6.62B
IMAX Corp.	NYSE: IMAX	Entertainment—Diversified	2.22B
Interclick	Acquired by Yahoo	Internet	–
Intercontinental Exchange, Inc.	NYSE: ICE	Diversified Investments	25.91 B
IVAX Corp.	Bought by Teva Pharma	Biopharma	–
Key Pharmaceuticals	Bought by Schering Plough	Biopharma	–
Kips Bay Medical Inc.	NASDAQ: KIPS	Medical Appliances & Equipment	432.48K
Manitex International Inc.	NASDAQ: MNTX	Diversified Machinery	107.30M
Market Leader Inc.	Acquired by Trulia	–	–
Medbox Inc.	OTCQB: MDBX	Machinery	7.96M
Medtronic Inc.	Medical Appliances & Equipment	NYSE: MDT	100.12B
Middleby Corp.	NASDAQ: MIDD	Diversified Machinery	6.30B
Mitcham Industries Inc.	NASDAQGS: MIND	Scientific & Tech Instruments	47.01M
Monster Beverage Corp.	NASDAQ: MNST	Beverages—Soft Drinks	28.13B
MusclePharm Corp.	OTCQB: MSLP	Personal Services	65.11M
New Park Resources Inc.	NSYE: NR	Oil/Gas Equipment & Services	553.69M
Nova Gold Resources Inc.	NYSE: NG	Gold	1.12B
Oculus Innovative Sciences Inc.	NASDAQ: OCLS	Drugs, Generic	18.87M
OPKO Health, Inc.	NYSE:OPK	Medical Appliances & Equipment	5.86B
Patrick Industries Inc.	NASDAQGS: PATK	Lumber, Wood Production	693.64M
Pershing Gold Corp.	NASDAQ: PGLC	Gold	100.72M
PharmAthene Inc.	NYSEMKT: PIP	Biotechnology	93.77M
Quadrant 4 Systems Corp.	OTCQB: QFOR	Information Tech—Services	30.90M
Revlon Inc.	NYSE: REV	Personal Products	1.72B
Sevion Therapeutics Inc.	OTCBB: SVON	Biotechnology	12.62M
Soltas	Private	Solar	–

Company	Ticker	Industry	Market Cap
Sorrento Therapeutics Inc.	NASDAQCM: SRNE	Biotechnology	499.59M
SpectraScience Inc.	OTC PINK: SCIE	Medical Appliances &Equipment	3.37M
Starbucks Corp.	NASDAQGS: SBUX	Specialty Eateries	81.94 B
St. Jude Medical Inc.	NYSE: STJ	Medical Appliances & Equipment	20.07B
Subway	Private	Food Service	–
Tesoro Oil	NYSE: TSO	Oil & Gas Refining & Marketing	11.81B
Teva Pharmaceutical Industries Limited	NYSE: TEVA	Drug Manufacturers, Other	53.86B
Texas Instruments, Inc.	NASDAQGS: TXN	Semiconductors, Broadline	49.97 B
Tulia Inc.	NYSE: TRLA	Internet Service Providers	1.72B
Virtus InvestmentPartners Inc.	NASDAQGS: VRTS	Asset Management	906.22B
Xplore Technologies Corp.	NASDAQCM: XPLR	Diversified Computer Systems	61.58M
Zagg Inc.	NASDAQGS: ZAGG	Specialty Retail, Other	214.65M
Zebra Technologies Corp.	NASDAQGS: ZBRA	Diversified Machinery	4.31B
VBI Vaccines	NASDAQ: VBIV	Biotechnology	60.34M
RealNetworks Inc.	NASDAQGS: RNWK	Technology	159.54M
*Immuron Ltd.	ASX	Biotechnology	37.48 M

*Listed in top 20 stocks 2015.

RedChip's Top Microcap Stock Picks

RedChip Top Picks: 2015

Company	Market	Ticker	Date Signed/ TV Interview	Initial Price	Price 1/1/2015	Current Price	Current % Gained
DS Healthcare Group	NASDAQCM	DSKX	10/9/2013	$1.89	$0.70	$3.69	427%
Immuron	ASX	IMC	7/20/2015	$0.27	$0.18	$0.50	178%
Bitcoin Shop	OTC QB	BTCS	4/25/2014	$0.36	$0.08	$0.21	163%
Oragenics	NYSE	OGEN	1/2/2014	$2.86	$0.86	$2.01	134%
Zivo Bioscience	OTC QB	ZIVO	8/21/2014	$0.14	$0.09	$0.17	89%
Northwest Biotherapeutics	NASDAQCM	NWBO	2/23/2013	$3.30	$5.42	$10.14	87%
Drone Aviation Holding	OTC QB	DRNE	8/1/2014	$0.56	$0.19	$0.31	63%
Zion Oil & Gas	NASDAQ	ZN	3/9/2015	$1.92	$1.38	$2.17	57%
OPKO Health	NYSE	OPK	1/9/2014	$8.43	$9.93	$15.21	53%
Direct Insite	OTC QB	DIRI	6/27/2013	$1.23	$0.75	$1.12	49%
RedHill Biopharma	NASDAQCM	RDHL	6/3/2014	$16.86	$13.79	$20.57	49%
Cancer Genetics	NASDAQCM	CGIX	4/30/2013	$11.40	$7.78	$11.55	48%
Apollo Medical Holdings	OTC QB	AMEH	2/23/2015	$4.30	$4.50	$6.50	44%
Ruthigen	NASDAQCM	RTGN	3/28/2014	$3.28	$3.52	$5.06	44%
AVG Technologies	NYSE	AVG	9/23/2014	$16.45	$19.58	$27.53	41%
Sorrento Therapeutics	NASDAQCM	SRNE	11/18/2013	$8.60	$10.16	$14.20	40%
SuperCom	NASDAQCM	SPCB	1/5/2015	$9.81	$9.81	$13.56	38%
Texas Rare Earth Resources	OTCQX	TRER	4/23/2015	$0.31	$0.21	$0.29	38%
ChromaDex	OTC QB	CDXC	6/3/2013	$0.71	$0.90	$1.19	32%

(Continued)

Company	Market	Ticker	Date Signed/ TV Interview	Initial Price	Price 1/1/2015	Current Price	Current % Gained
Attunity	NASDAQCM	ATTU	1/8/2015	$10.52	$10.61	$13.33	26%
Biocept	NASDAQCM	BIOC	4/24/2014	$5.00	$2.48	$2.99	21%

*Current price may vary on certain stocks. Most current prices were on July 8, 2015.

RedChip Top Picks: 2012–2014

RedChip Top Performers 2012–2014

Company	Date Signed/ TV Interview	Initial Price	Highest Closing Price	*Current Price	*Current % Gained	Highest % Gained
Quadrant 4 Systems (OTCQB: QFOR)	8/12/2013	$0.06	$1.38	$0.50	733%	2200%
Inovio Pharmaceuticals (NYSE-MKT: INO)	11/17/2012	$1.96	$15.28	$11.03	463%	680%
Profire Energy (NASDAQ CM: PFIE)	8/7/2013	$1.40	$5.78	$3.85	175%	313%
Galectin Therapeutics (NASDAQ CM: GALT)	6/13/2012	$2.00	$18.30	$4.90	145%	815%
Craft Brew Alliance (NASDAQGS: BREW)	12/15/2012	$6.49	$17.78	$15.06	132%	174%
MusclePharm (OTCQB: MSLP)	2/8/2013	$6.49	$13.80	$13.35	106%	113%
Giggles n' Hugs (OTCQB: GIGL)	5/6/2014	$0.28	$1.43	$0.53	89%	411%
InterCloud Systems (NASDAQ CM: ICLD)	11/11/2013	$2.47	$18.36	$4.53	83%	643%

Company	Date Signed/ TV Interview	Initial Price	Highest Closing Price	*Current Price	*Current % Gained	Highest % Gained
Vapor Corp. (OTCQB: VPCO)	6/07/2013	$3.35	$9.80	$1.65	−51%	193%
Northwest Biotherapeutics (NASDAQ CM: NWBO)	2/23/2013	$3.30	$9.18	$5.38	63%	178%
OxySure Systems, Inc. (OTCQB: OXYS)	9/02/2014	$0.72	$1.20	$1.20	66%	66%
Asure Software (NASDAQ CM: ASUR)	12/12/2011	$3.17	$7.91	$4.90	55%	150%
Trecora Resources (NYSE: TREC)	3/23/2013	$8.32	$13.39	$12.20	47%	61%
Galaxy Gaming, Inc. (OTCBB: GLXZ)	6/13/2013	$0.27	$0.50	$0.39	44%	85%
Cancer Genetics, Inc. (NASDAQ CM: CGIX)	4/30/2013	$11.40	$21.00	$7.98	−30%	84%
American Water Works (NYSE: AWK)	1/19/2013	$37.91	$50.61	$48.19	27%	34%
BDCA Venture (NASDAQ CM: BDCV)	4/27/2013	$3.95	$7.30	$4.81	22%	85%
Lightbridge (NASDAQ CM: LTBR)	10/15/2012	$2.00	$3.75	$2.31	16%	88%
Xplore Technologies (NASDAQ CM: XPLR)	12/5/2012	$4.30	$7.30	$4.73	10%	70%
Digital Cinema Destinations (NASDAQ CM: DCIN)	7/2/2013	$5.49	$6.78	$5.99	9%	23%

*Current price may vary on certain stocks. Most current prices were recorded from period October 1, 2014, through November 20, 2014.

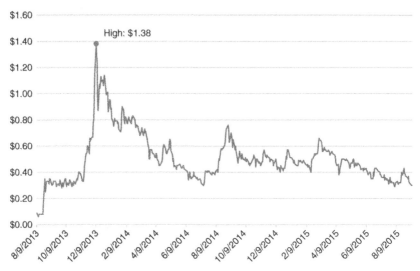

FIGURE B.1 Quadrant 4 Systems (OTCQB: QFOR)
Data Source: Thomson Reuters Corporation.

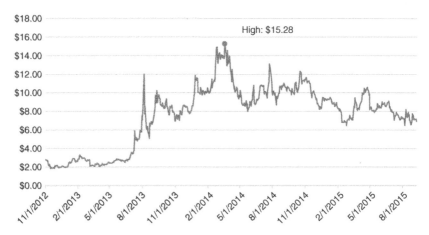

FIGURE B.2 Inovio Pharmaceuticals (NYSE: INO)
Data Source: Thomson Reuters Corporation.

FIGURE B.3 Profire Energy (NASDAQ: PFIE)
Data Source: Thomson Reuters Corporation.

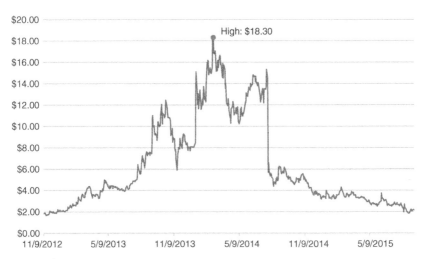

FIGURE B.4 Galectin Therapeutics (NASDAQ: GALT)
Data Source: Thomson Reuters Corporation.

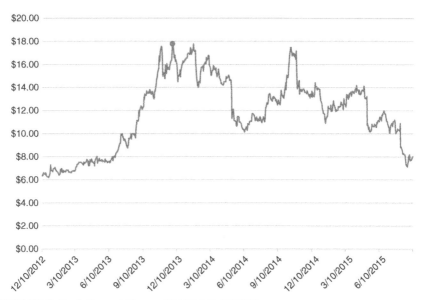

FIGURE B.5 Craft Brew Alliance (NASDAQ: BREW)
Data Source: Thomson Reuters Corporation.

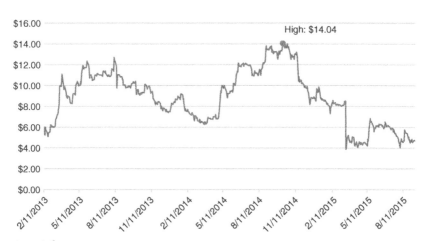

FIGURE B.6 RedChip first featured MusclePharm (OTC: MSLP) on February 8, 2013
Data Source: Thomson Reuters Corporation.

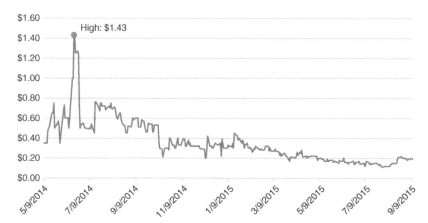

FIGURE B.7 RedChip first featured Giggles N' Hugs (OTC: GIGL) on May 6, 2014
Data Source: Thomson Reuters Corporation.

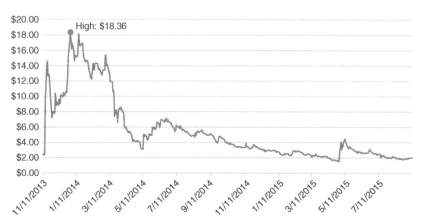

FIGURE B.8 RedChip first featured InterCloud Systems (NASDAQ: ICLD) on
November 11, 2013
Data Source: Thomson Reuters Corporation.

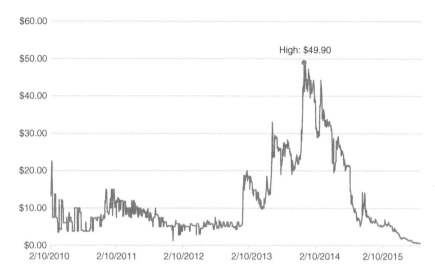

FIGURE B.9 RedChip first featured Vapor Corp. (NASDAQ: VPCO) on February 10, 2010
Data Source: Thomson Reuters Corporation.

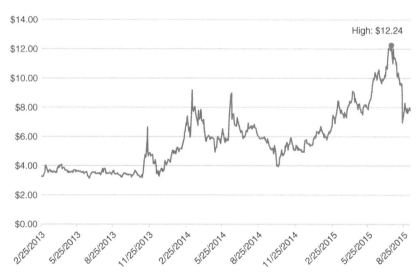

FIGURE B.10 RedChip first featured Northwest Biotherapeutics (NASDAQ: NWBO) on February 23, 2013
Data Source: Thomson Reuters Corporation.

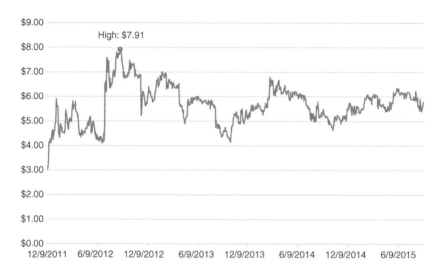

FIGURE B.11 RedChip first featured Asure Software (NASDAQ: ASUR) on December 12, 2011
Data Source: Thomson Reuters Corporation.

FIGURE B.12 RedChip first featured Trecora Resources (NYSE: TREC) on March 23, 2013
Data Source: Thomson Reuters Corporation.

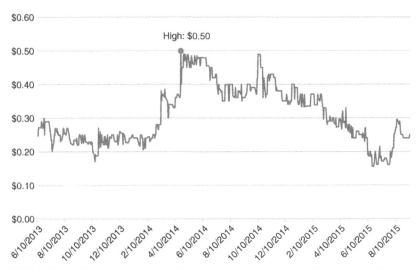

FIGURE B.13 RedChip first featured Galaxy Gaming (OTC: GLXZ) on June 13, 2013
Data Source: Thomson Reuters Corporation.

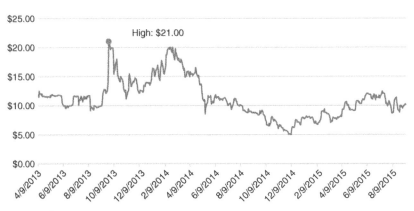

FIGURE B.14 RedChip first featured Cancer Genetics (NASDAQ: CGIX) on April 30, 2013
Data Source: Thomson Reuters Corporation.

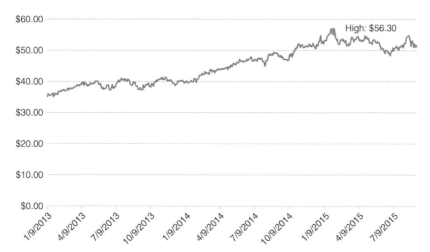

FIGURE B.15 RedChip first featured American Water Works (NYSE: AWK) on January 19, 2013

Data Source: Thomson Reuters Corporation.

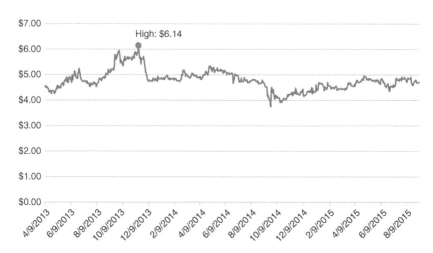

FIGURE B.16 RedChip first featured BDCA Venture (NASDAQ: BDCV) on April 27, 2013

Data Source: Thomson Reuters Corporation.

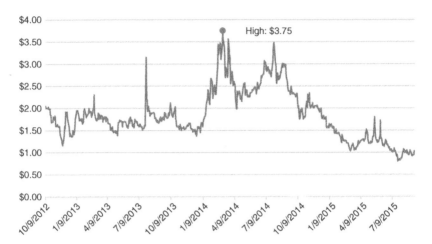

FIGURE B.17 RedChip first featured Lightbridge (NASDAQ: LTBR) on October 15, 2012

Data Source: Thomson Reuters Corporation.

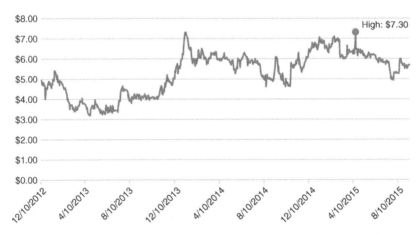

FIGURE B.18 RedChip first featured Xplore Technologies (NASDAQ: XPLR) on December 5, 2012

Data Source: Thomson Reuters Corporation.

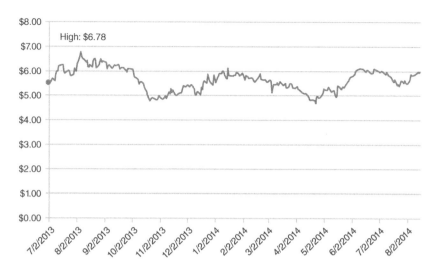

FIGURE B.19 RedChip first featured Digital Cinema Destinations (NASDAQ: DCIN) on July 2, 2013

Data Source: Thomson Reuters Corporation.

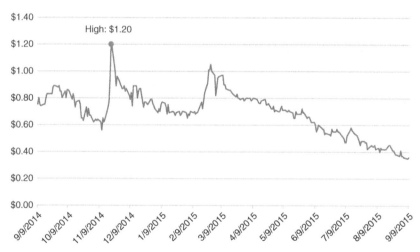

FIGURE B.20 RedChip first featured OxySure Systems (OTC: OXYS) on September 2, 2014

Data Source: Thomson Reuters Corporation.

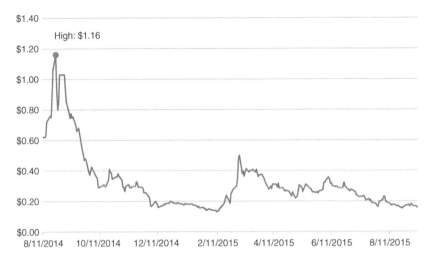

FIGURE B.21 RedChip first featured Drone Aviation Corp. (OTC: DRNE) on
August 1, 2014

Data Source: Thomson Reuters Corporation.

RedChip Top Picks: 2005–2011

RedChip Top Performers 2012–2014

Company	Date Research Issued	Initial Price	Highest Closing Price	Closing Price 10/8/2014	Current % Gained	Highest % Gained
Newtek Business Services, Inc (NASDAQ: NEWT)	2/10/06	$1.75	$3.36	$2.68	53.1%	92.0%
Greenfield Online, Inc. (NASDAQ: SRVY)	10/24/05	$4.91	$18.19	–	–	270.5%
Pervasive Software, Inc. (NASDAQ: PVSW)	12/19/05	$4.14	$9.20	–	–	122.2%
Diamond Foods, Inc. (NASDAQ: DMND)	3/13/09	$22.23	$92.28	$28.80	29.6%	315.1%
LKQ Corporation (NASDAQ: LKQ)	11/28/05	$17.00	$33.86	$26.66	56.8%	99.2%
Inventure Foods, Inc. (NASDAQ: SNAK)	7/14/10	$3.06	$14.28	$13.08	327.5%	366.7%

Company	Date Research Issued	Initial Price	Highest Closing Price	Closing Price 10/8/2014	Current % Gained	Highest % Gained
OptionsXpress, Inc. (NASDAQ: OXPS)	1/18/06	$28.44	$33.90	–	–	19.2%
Antares Pharma, Inc. (NASDAQ: ATRS)	9/16/10	$1.49	$5.32	$1.97	32.2%	257.0%
Yak Communications (NASDAQ: YAKC)	2/28/06	$3.28	$5.23	–	–	59.5%
Boots & Coots (NASDAQ: WEL)	6/06/06	$1.67	$3.15	–	–	88.6%
Limoneira Company (NASDAQ: LMNR)	7/14/10	$17.77	$28.34	$24.05	35.3%	59.5%
CytRx Corporation (NASDAQ: CYTR)	6/03/08	$0.94	$9.87	$2.51	167.0%	950.0%
ZAGG, Inc. (NASDAQ: ZAGG)	6/04/09	$5.45	$16.62	$5.51	1.1%	205.0%
Craft Brewers Alliance, Inc. (NASDAQ: BREW)	7/14/10	$4.94	$17.78	$15.76	219.0%	259.9%
Sharps Compliance, Inc. (NASDAQ: SMED)	2/13/08	$2.25	$11.91	$4.34	92.9%	429.3%

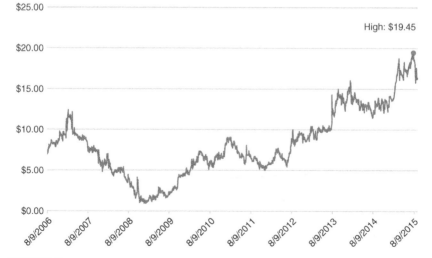

FIGURE B.22 RedChip research coverage issued on February 10, 2006
Data Source: Thomson Reuters Corporation.

FIGURE B.23 RedChip research coverage issued on October 24, 2005
Data Source: Thomson Reuters Corporation.

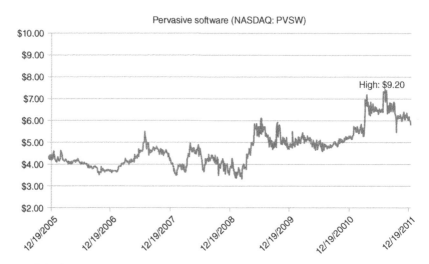

FIGURE B.24 RedChip research coverage issued on December 19, 2005
Data Source: Thomson Reuters Corporation.

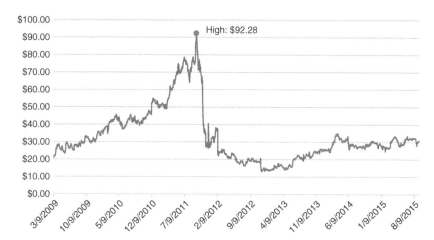

FIGURE B.25 RedChip research coverage issued on March 13, 2009
Data Source: Thomson Reuters Corporation.

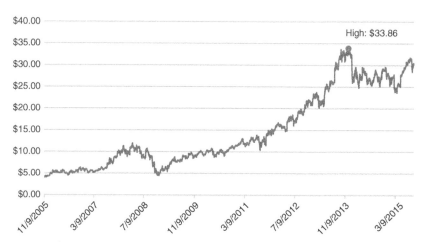

FIGURE B.26 RedChip research coverage issued on November 28, 2005
Data Source: Thomson Reuters Corporation.

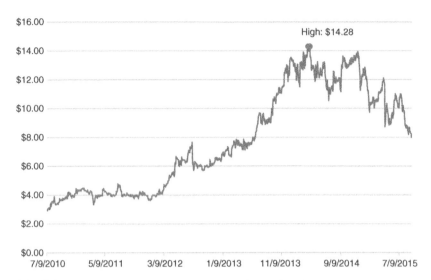

FIGURE B.27 RedChip research coverage issued on July 14, 2010
Data Source: Thomson Reuters Corporation.

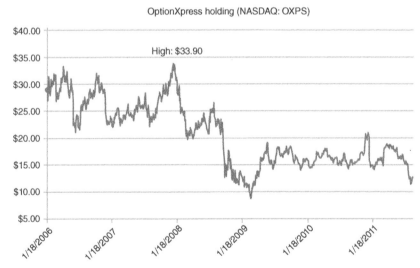

FIGURE B.28 RedChip research coverage issued on January 18, 2006
Data Source: Thomson Reuters Corporation.

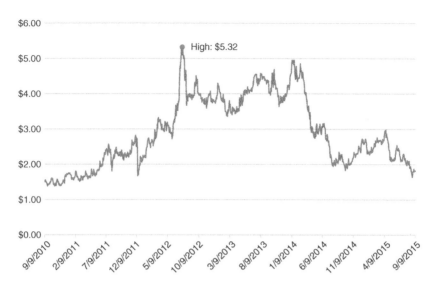

FIGURE B.29 RedChip research coverage issued on September 16, 2010
Data Source: Thomson Reuters Corporation.

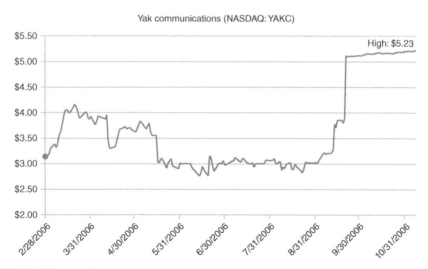

FIGURE B.30 RedChip research coverage issued on February 28, 2006
Data Source: Thomson Reuters Corporation.

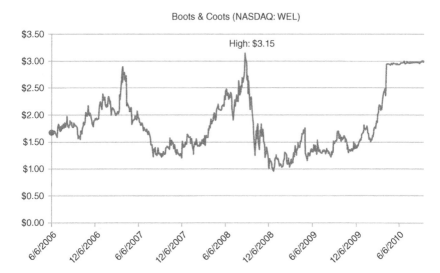

FIGURE B.31 RedChip research coverage issued on June 6, 2006
Data Source: Thomson Reuters Corporation.

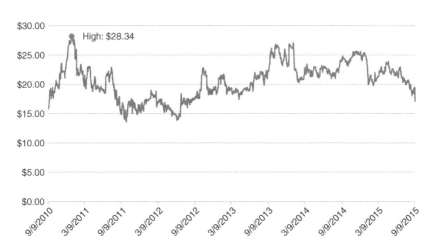

FIGURE B.32 RedChip first featured Limoneira Company on July 14, 2010
Data Source: Thomson Reuters Corporation.

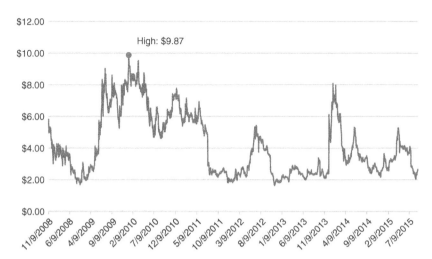

FIGURE B.33 RedChip research coverage issued on June 3, 2008
Data Source: Thomson Reuters Corporation.

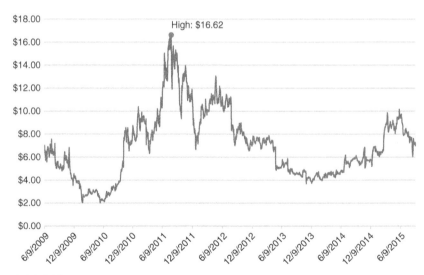

FIGURE B.34 RedChip research coverage issued on June 4, 2009
Data Source: Thomson Reuters Corporation.

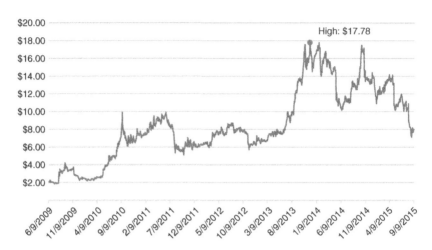

FIGURE B.35 RedChip research coverage issued on July 14, 2010
Data Source: Thomson Reuters Corporation.

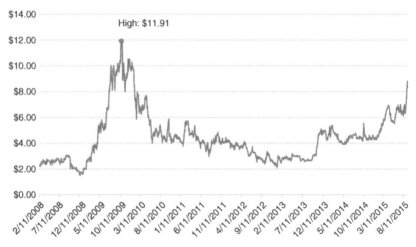

FIGURE B.36 RedChip research coverage issued on February 13, 2008
Data Source: Thomson Reuters Corporation.

Lessons from RedChip Nation: Weekly Newsletter

The following lessons are selected from RedChip's weekly newsletter, *The RedChip Money Report.*

A Random Walk in the Markets

One of the many ideas that the book, *Against the Gods, the Remarkable Story of Risk*, contemplates is whether stock prices "follow a random walk—that they resemble the aimless and unplanned lurches of a drunk trying to grab hold of a lamppost," or do they have a memory and thus follow a predictable pattern. The authors make a few simple observations regarding the debate:

1. The capital markets are fluid and competitive.
2. Investors are engaged in a war of wits, trying to outsmart each other.
3. New information is rapidly reflected in the price of stocks.
4. New information arrives in random fashion.
5. Investors sometimes interpret data differently.
6. Investors have different reasons for buying, holding, or selling.

Conclusion: Stock prices move in unpredictable ways.

Here is what we do know, according to the authors of the book: The stock market on average has gone up. "From January 1926 to December 1995 the Standard and Poor's Index of 500 stocks saw an average annual increase of 7.7% (excluding dividends)." In 47 of the 70 years in the period studied, stocks went up. But what the study reveals is that "the stock market record" is more like a "random walk" than a predictable preplanned

25-mile run, as after correcting "for the upward drift," changes in the S&P 500 were as likely to be upward as downward over the 70-year period.

Volatility: Opportunity and Risk

The broader markets, after reaching record highs earlier this month, came under severe selling pressure last week. Many small stocks succumbed to the wave of selling. In this type of environment, it's very important to keep perspective of why you bought specific companies in the first place. Are those reasons still valid? Has anything changed to warrant a selloff in a particular name? Oftentimes, in the short term, small stocks move for reasons beyond the merits of the individual companies themselves. If it's broad market selling pressure that's wreaking havoc on a position, but the merits of that particular company are still valid and improving, this type of volatility can present a great opportunity to accumulate shares at a discount.

On the other hand, if the fundamental picture has changed for a particular company, it's time to take inventory of the reasons you originally picked up the shares. Has the story changed to the point that your original reasons for ownership are no longer valid? In such cases, you may need to consider selling the position. Oftentimes, though, the ills of the broader market are relatively unrelated to the potential of smaller stocks. Smaller stocks are typically growth oriented, taking market share from huge market opportunities. This is vastly different than a Fortune 100 multinational trying to maintain large market share on a global basis. Because of this, smaller stocks can often weather the storms of the broader market and bounce back very quickly. So, bottom line, do your due diligence, know why you own a position, keep an eye out for shifting dynamics, and don't let the volatility of the broader market shake you out of the right positions.

Relative Value

When buying any stock, we're always interested in getting "a good price," and in the case of buying small caps, price is often the critical factor in a winning investment. But what is a good price? To determine if a stock is trading at a good price, we need to look at its relative value to its peers. To do this, we can compare various ratios, like price-to-sales, price-to-earnings, price-to-book, and other metrics. Depending on the industry and stage of growth, certain ratios can be more important than others. You can look at research reports on peer companies to see which ratios analysts put more importance on for the specific industry you are looking at. By doing the extra homework, you'll be in a better position to determine if you're getting a good price.

Finding Opportunity in Disaster and Turmoil

Sophisticated and successful investors often find opportunity when others are gripped by fear. Not long ago, in early 2009, as the average investor was throwing in the towel at the nadir of the financial crisis, BlackRock, Pimco, and other major funds were stepping back into the market and taking advantage of the firesale. Stock market history is replete with similar examples of big investors making the right moves in the wake of turmoil while the masses made the wrong moves.

While it's too early to know how the current geopolitical risk and uncertainties surrounding the situation in the Ukraine will play out, there are recent past events that have run their course and could provide investors with substantial rewards.

One such case is what is transpiring in the uranium markets. In 2011, in the wake of the tsunami that devastated Japan, uranium markets, and their related stocks, took a substantial and prolonged beating. It has taken several years for the dust to settle, but now things look poised for significant upside. Strengthening the case for uranium is the recent expiration of the Highly Enriched Uranium Agreement with Russia, which removed 25 million pounds, roughly half of current U.S. consumption, from the global supply. One benefactor of this seismic shift in market dynamics is Energy Fuels (NYSE MKT: UUUU), the largest conventional uranium miner in the United States. The stock has already moved up 100% since the expiration of the pact, but is still trading at just a small fraction of its pre–Japanese crisis levels. While other investors have either moved on to other markets or are still fearful of the future prospects for uranium, smart sophisticated investors are beginning to recognize the changes underway and are positioned for big gains in the months and quarters ahead.

Small-Cap Investors Need to Take Risks to Gain Rewards

As investors, we're always making decisions that try to find the right balance between risk and reward. In the small-cap markets in particular, the rewards can be substantial. Of course, the inverse of that is small-caps can lose significant value as well. To balance that risk and position yourself for the substantial rewards available from the right opportunities it's important you properly diversify among a basket of small-caps. Don't put all your small-cap money in just one or two stocks. Instead, spread your investment money out over a larger number of stocks and keep constant watch for changes in the reasons behind why you acquired each stock. When things change for the worse, don't be afraid to take your losses. Additionally, when selecting which stocks to buy, look for strong businesses that address large unmet market needs and try to find opportunities that are immune to broader market swings. These are the types of things we look for here at RedChip, and our impressive track record is a testament to the fact that it works.

Leadership Makes or Breaks Companies

You can have a great technology, a great product or service, but with the wrong management team, or with the wrong CEO, things can go really wrong. Jim Collins's book, *Good to Great*, talks about level 5 leaders and their qualities. One of the qualities of great leaders is humility, a lack of hubris, a willingness to give others credit and to admit when one is wrong. All the great companies in Jim Collins's book had level 5 leaders. Collins defined great companies as those that outperformed the market by at least three times over a 15-year period.

Capitalism: Greed, Recklessness, and Self-Interest

We cannot control the greed, the self-interest, or the recklessness of investors who have positioned or funded the companies we bring to you. Case in point: The first time I gave you a company called Spherix (NASDAQ: SPEX) it was trading at $7.33, on April 6, 2013. The stock went on a rocket ride, closing at $21.70 four months later on August 6, 2013. Of course the stock did not hold the high. The stock retraced to the $10.00–$11.00 range and then a few months later, a massive selloff occurred from those who held stock with less than a $1.00 cost average, the founders, and previous shell owners. They could have exited the stock at $10.00 or more, as the stock was trading hundreds of thousands of shares a day, but greed and stupidity led them to sell it down to under $3.00.

The Importance of Proper Funding

Microcaps are by their very nature less developed companies with much shorter track records than their mid-cap and big-cap brethren. Things can change dramatically in a day or a week for some of these stocks. One of the most important and obvious things we look for is whether the company is properly capitalized, and if not, do they have the ability to get funded in a way that will allow them to execute on their business plans. One of the problems with smaller companies is that they sometimes raise capital on terms that are not favorable to the shareholders, and that is so heavily discounted or structured in a way that could leave the stock trading well below its peer group average for years, even if they are executing brilliantly.

These are what we call broken stocks and until someone steps in and cleans up the stock, takes out the old investors, and restructures the company, the stock goes nowhere.

High-Speed Trading

There is an army on Wall Street of high-frequency traders who know what you want to buy and how much before your order to buy is filled. Their systems are faster by milliseconds, just enough to buy the shares being offered for sale in Microsoft or Facebook, for example, before your order is executed so that they can buy them ahead of you, drive the price up, and sell them back to you at a higher price in less than the blink of an eye. Read Michael Lewis's new book, *Flash Boys*, for an in-depth look at this phenomenon.

Big Gain Potential in Small-Cap Stocks

Microcap pros buy stocks before they get liquid, while they are quiet, and eventually sell high to make millions. They do their homework, find stocks that are truly undervalued in their peer group, and quietly begin accumulating. They are patient. They may be in a stock six months or three years before the broader market takes an interest. Take Quadrant 4 Systems (OTCQB: QFOR), for example. This company first joined the RedChip Nation in August 2013. When this company signed with RedChip they were trading at six cents with very little volume. The stock is now trading at 0.38, down significantly from a high of $1.38 in December of 2013. It stands as a shining example of the extraordinary gains that can be achieved investing in the small-cap space. It also, once again, illustrates the point that microcaps are the most volatile asset class.

Measuring Volatility

Investors can assess a stock's volatility by checking its BETA coefficient. BETA measures a company's stock volatility compared to the overall market. A stock with a BETA of 1 is expected to move in tandem with the market or be equally as volatile as the market. Stocks with BETAs lower than 1 are less volatile than the market, and the lower the number, the higher the chance of preserving your capital. Stocks with BETAs higher than 1 are considered to be more volatile than the market and will rise and fall faster. If you're looking for stocks with higher risk and higher rewards, you should study stocks with higher BETA numbers.

Buy Companies, Not Stocks

Words of wisdom from Byron Roth, CEO and chairman of ROTH Capital Partners:

1. "Buy companies, not stocks; if you buy stocks, it will drive you crazy; when the market drops, illiquid microcap stocks are going to get hurt badly, so always remember that you're buying a company."
2. "If you watch the market every day, the stock will drive you crazy."
3. "You can be happy with the companies you own, but not their stock."
4. "If you invest and you know what you're investing in, you'll have your day when the market recognizes, but it might not be today or tomorrow."
5. "Have a private equity mentality and take a concentrated position and don't worry what the mark is at the end of the quarter; just know what you're getting into."
6. "When no one wants the stock, that's often the best time to buy. Some of my best institutions buy when everything is out of favor."

The Importance of Liquidity in Smaller-Cap Stocks

By liquidity we mean how many shares the stock trades per day. Liquidity is determined by a number of factors: the number of shares in the float, or the number of shares held by the public that can be bought and sold. Typically, most companies do not have all of their shares outstanding in the public float; shares could be locked up from financings, or a percentage may be held by insiders. Most stockbrokers will advise you not to buy a stock that is not liquid. Most big-cap stocks trade between 2% and 5% of their float per day. Some of the smartest microcap fund managers say that they "like to buy stocks before they are liquid, before anyone else finds out about them." The reason is simple: By the time everyone else understands and appreciates the value proposition of the company, the stock will theoretically have started trading near or at its true value.

Factors Affecting Liquidity
- The number of shares available to trade; the size of the public float
- The number of shareholders and the amount that each holds
- The price at which the larger position holders are willing to sell

By way of example, if stock xyz is trading at $2.80, and a potential seller will not sell below $3.50, and he owns a controlling block or a relatively large percentage of the float, this factor alone could inhibit trading in the stock.

Buying Smaller-Cap Stocks Poses Risks

Microcaps are the most volatile asset class. Best to buy smaller-caps in bunches. The proverbial "Don't put all your eggs in one basket" is a cardinal principle when investing in speculative stocks. Even the most promising, well-researched companies sometimes throw investors curve balls, causing stocks to retrace gains and putting a stay on big returns for years. With a basket of smaller stocks, you mitigate risk, balancing your portfolio with stocks that may be in an upward trajectory while others may be flat.

Defensive Stocks

Defensive stocks are stocks that are usually immune to the ups and downs of the economy and tend to be less risky than cyclical stocks. Defensive stocks have stability in their earnings and stable markets for their products. Some defensive stock groups include tobacco, food, and drugs. Investors should consider these stocks when anticipating a market downturn. While we're certainly not predicting a downturn at this time, an example of a defensive stock from the biotechnology space is Cancer Genetics (NASDAQ: CGIX), an emerging leader in DNA-based cancer diagnostics with over seven tests in development that provide diversification and risk reduction.

Be a Contrarian!

There's not much of a reward in betting with the crowd. If you want a significant return on an investment, you've got to be willing to bet against the crowd. If a company is doing poorly, most think it will continue to do poorly, or vice versa—a company doing well will continue to do so. Be cautious and don't confuse good businesses with good investments. They're not always one and the same. Investors' expectations usually are built into a stock price, and you'll be rewarded if you understand that when expectations change, so will the price of the stock.

What Insider Buying May Tell Us

Insider buying is a screen many institutions use to determine whether a stock may be a buy. Insider buying may be a sign that management believes the stock is undervalued at current levels. Insider buying may also be used to bolster or strengthen the stock. Either way, one can find situations that warrant attention.

When to Sell

One of the hardest decisions small-cap investors face is knowing when and why to sell a stock. Monitoring a stock for changes in earnings and revenues should be done frequently. Changes in a company's fundamentals and other announcements can signal a modification in a company's growth. Wall Street may view a lack of growth as a loss of credibility or momentum and send your stock lower. Put a limit on your stock losses; if you are down big and the reasons you own the stock have changed, cut your losses and sell. On the flip-side, when should we take a profit? An old saying comes to mind: "Pigs get fat and hogs get slaughtered." Same idea here. Place a profit in mind and sell when you've made a specific gain, or sell enough to cover your original cost and the rest is gravy. Know your limits and practice discipline.

Constant Dollar Plan

A constant dollar plan, also known as dollar-cost averaging, is an investment strategy that's useful for accumulating shares of one company over time. Under the system, you invest a fixed amount of capital on a routine basis regardless of how many shares your money will buy. You'll buy more shares when the price is low and fewer shares when the price is high.

Warning from a Top Lawyer in the Microcap Space

"There are lots of players looming in the shadows to hurt small public companies. You have to learn how to separate the good from the bad. It's easier to perpetrate fraud in the microcap sector than it is with the bigger companies. Watch out for shell promoters, nominee accounts, hidden stock accounts among those who own stocks in shells" (Greg Sichenzia, founder of Sichenzia Ross Friedman Ference LLP).

Technical Analysis

Technical analysis can be helpful in determining when to buy a stock or sell a stock, but as a system, technical analysis is overrated and far from perfect, particularly when it comes to rating smaller-caps. I have seen technicals that indicated "Strong Buy" and the stock proceeded to move southward. Always examine the balance sheet and the income statement of any company before purchasing the stock. Look at the management team. What is their history of experience in the industry the company operates in? Are there industry pros on their board of directors? Be sure the company has enough cash to fund operations for the next 12 months, and if not, determine whether they are capable of getting funding by examining their 10-Qs and 8-Ks for past fundings.

Averaging Down

One should average down on a stock only when the fundamentals are strong or at minimum getting better. Smaller-cap stocks can drop 10%–15% in a day for no apparent fundamental reason. A fund or a large position holder may decide to exit the stock for reasons unrelated to the company's future prospects. The exiting investor may simply need capital or believes the stock is not going higher in the short term. ZAGG (NASDAQ: ZAGG) is a stock that illustrates my point well. The stock has been trading between $6.80 and $8.00 for months. The stock has a tendency to run up to between $7.80 and $8.00 a share, then pull back within days or weeks to the low $7.00 range. In fact, the stock in recent days made a move from around $7.20 to $7.60, a 5% gain in just a few days. The fundamentals on this company remain strong. This is a good stock to buy on the dips or average down. One can trade this stock and make 10% in the short term or hold the stock for the longer term for a much larger gain.

Look for Companies with Low Price-to-Earnings Ratios

Study companies in an industry and determine which ones are still trading inefficiently, lower than their peer-group P/E multiples. Next, check their year-over-year and quarterly earnings and revenue growth. Go back at least eight quarters and look for trends, consistency, or inconsistencies in their year-over-year and quarterly growth rates. If the fundamentals are stable and there are no indications that their business is faltering, then chances are the stock, at some point in time, will trade somewhere near the peer-group P/E average.

Management Is the First Fundamental

Management is the first fundamental to consider when evaluating smaller-cap companies. In *Good to Great*, Jim Collins discovered that in the companies that made the transition from good-to-great, outperforming the market by at least three times over a 15-year period, the quality the CEOs all possessed was humility: the capacity to admit mistakes and consider new ideas while habitually giving others the credit. Of course, the great company CEOs had many other qualities that contributed to their success, including the ability to keep their companies focused on their core businesses, the businesses they could be the best at in their space. Be careful of companies that announce acquisitions that are not in their core business segments. Look closely at management's background, their history of achievement or nonachievement at previous enterprises in which they were involved. And remember, hubris at the top is rarely a good sign for small companies trying to grow.

Stay Away from China Stocks Listed in the United States

I was once a defender of the China small-cap space. RedChip spent seven years working in China small-caps, representing dozens of companies. However, over the past 12 months I have come to the conclusion that the financial fraud among Chinese companies listed in the United States is more pervasive than I previously thought. Billion-dollar market-cap companies with Big Four auditors, such as SinoForest and Longtop Financial, were determined to have submitted fraudulent financial statements to the SEC. Billions of dollars of investor money has been deployed in U.S.-listed Chinese companies, both big and small, too many of which were later found to be perpetrating fraud, siphoning off investor dollars into their own hands while falsifying bank statements, deceiving even the biggest and best auditing firms.

Meanwhile, Chinese authorities refuse to allow the Public Company Accounting Oversight Board to inspect the work of Chinese auditors who review and sign off on financial statements. My position now is that investors should not invest one penny in any China company listed in the United States. In fact I have grown more nationalistic and would now consider myself a critic of China policy and practice. China continues to steal technology from the United States, costing us billions of dollars and thousands of jobs. The cost of Chinese copyright infringement and pirated goods, including software, shoes, cigarettes, DVDs, and sophisticated weapons system technology, is an enormous problem for the United States. This is just one more reason to take your money out of Chinese stocks.

We have enough fast growing smaller-cap companies here in the United States that deserve your investment dollar. China entrepreneurs simply do not deserve our investment dollars. Those Chinese business owners who have committed fraud against U.S. investors have ruined it for their honest brethren. Stay away from China stocks listed in the United States.

Let the Winners Run

As I interviewed for this book one theme that kept emerging was, to use the words of Michael Corbett of Perritt Capital Management, one must learn to "let the winners run." Too often investors employ a short-term horizon to microcap investing. If the stock is working and the company is executing, then do not be so quick to take a 50% profit when, if you wait another year or two, you could have a 300% to 500% return.

Look for Stocks with Insider Buying

Look for stocks with insider buying, but not gimmick insider buying. By gimmick buying, I mean an officer or director who buys a thousand or a few thousand shares for window dressing, as if to trick us into believing he or she is buying for good reason. We want to find stocks with consistent and significant insider buying, buying that is the product of officers, directors, and management truly believing their stock is undervalued.

Here are three stocks with insider buying in the past 90 days:
1. Suffolk Bancorp (NASDAQ: SUBK), $163.32M market cap
2. Tetraphase Pharmaceuticals (NASDAQ: TTPH), $142.45M market cap
3. ValueVision Media, Inc. (NASDAQ: VVTV), $163.14M market cap

Value Investing

Value investing is an approach that originated about 70 years ago from the godfather of the method, Benjamin Graham. Graham's value investing influenced Warren Buffett and is still used today by many individuals and institutional investors. Value investing puts emphasis on tangible assets, earnings, dividends, financial strength and stability, as well as quality of management. In a nutshell, value investors believe that they should buy stocks with undervalued assets and eventually those assets will appreciate to their true value in the marketplace. We should note that intelligent value investing also consists of examining potential purchases according to healthy business practices and sticking to your own decisions without being influenced by the market.

What Is Beta: RedChip Nation Stocks' Beta Rankings

Beta is a measurement for analyzing a stock's volatility. Beta is used by some investment professionals to determine a stock's volatility relative to the general market. A stock's beta is typically measured against the S&P 500

Index. The beta of the S&P 500 is 1.00. A beta of 1.40 means that the stock theoretically could move down or up as much as 40% more than the general market. Low-beta stocks are purchased by some investment managers when the market outlook is less than positive or highly volatile. High-beta stocks are purchased when the outlook for the market is positive. The problem with using beta to determine which stocks to buy is that like all technical analysis, it is not foolproof. Smaller-cap stocks, as the most volatile asset class, have the highest beta. They are particularly difficult to analyze using beta because some of the issues are thinly traded. Jeffrey B. Little and Lucien Rhodes make the point in *Understanding Wall Street* that "beta never remains constant and that predicting its future direction can be hazardous. For example, bank stocks were once thought to be low-beta issues, which has not been the case in more recent years."

Capital Gains

When making investments in small-caps, it's easy to focus on your risk tolerance and return goals, but don't forget to assess your tax exposure on your winners. What's left after taxes is really what counts. Capital gains will kick in on any profits you make from the sale of stocks where the sale price exceeds the purchase price. Keep track of the dates you make purchases, and review them prior to making a sale. Knowing your time horizons can make a difference to your wallet. Short-term gains are those holding periods of a year or less that are taxed at higher tax rates than a long-term gain (more than one year). Holding a position for a bit more time may be to your advantage. The IRS is watching your trading time horizons—are you?

Symbols with 5 Letters

Sometimes we run into stocks that have five letters in their symbols. Here's a letter list explaining what each one references:

- A: Class A stock
- B: Class B stock
- C: Exempt from NASDAQ listing requirements for a limited period of time
- D: A new issue of an existing stock (usually the result of a reverse split)
- E: Delinquent in required filings with the SEC as determined by the NASD

F: Foreign
G: First convertible bond
H: Second convertible bond, same company
I: Third convertible bond, same company
J: Voting stock
K: Nonvoting stock
L: Miscellaneous situations such as foreign preferred, etc.
M: Fourth preferred stock
N: Third preferred stock
O: Second preferred stock
P: First preferred stock
Q: In bankruptcy proceedings
R: Rights
S: Beneficial interest shares
T: With warrants or with rights
U: Units
V: When-issued and when-distributed
W: Warrants
X: Mutual fund
Y: ADR (American depositary receipts)
Z: Miscellaneous

97% of Fund Managers Don't Generate Enough Returns to Cover the Expenses They Charge

The opening paragraph of Jason Zweig's blog on WSJ.com, commenting on the 2013 Nobel Prize winners in economics, titled: "The Nobel Prize Is No Crystal Ball," is sobering: "For investors, the main lesson from this week's announcement of the Nobel Prize in economics should be humility about anyone's market-forecasting—especially your own."

The three economists who won the coveted prize have spent their careers studying the financial markets. A disturbing finding by Professor Eugene Fama, one of the recipients, who teaches at the University of Chicago's Booth School of Business, is that 97% of fund managers do not generate enough returns to cover their fees. That should give all of us pause for thought. Though there seems to be sufficient evidence that demonstrates small stocks do outperform the market historically (see previous quote), a simple but important lesson emerges from the work of three remarkable men: Diversify your assets and by all means do not entrust your money to one fund or the ideas of any one person.

Financial Reporting Requirements

Federal securities law requires that public companies regularly report their financial conditions. This is done through three quarterly reports (SEC Form 10-Q) and one annual report (SEC Form 10-K) each fiscal year. These reports provide comprehensive information about a company's business and financial condition.

The SEC has different reporting deadlines for different companies. Larger companies (known as accelerated filers) have to complete their filings first. Smaller-reporting companies (with less than $75 million floats) are given up to 45 days from the end of a quarter to file Form 10-Q and up to 90 days from the end of a fiscal year to file Form 10-K.

If a company doesn't meet the initial deadline, they can request a 10-day extension. At the end of the extension period, if the company is still delinquent in its filing, the SEC will append an "E" to the stock symbol. Once the company completes its SEC filing the "E" will drop back off and the stock will continue trading under its original ticker.

While all smaller reporting companies have the same amount of time to complete the quarterly and annual filings, not all of these companies have the same deadline. This is because different companies can have different fiscal years. One company may have a fiscal year that ends in January. Another may have a fiscal year that ends in August. Keep that in mind as you try to determine when a particular company may be expected to report its earnings.

Analysts Can't Be Right All the Time

Most investors don't realize that Wall Street analysts are wrong more than they are right. At the big investment banks, we find analysts putting "Buy" ratings on stocks after their institutional desks have built their positions, giving the ball to the retail brokers to put their clients in as the institutions are profiting from the rise in the stock. Best to get in a stock before the traditional Wall Street analyst discovers it. Find stocks that the pack is not thinking about, but that have strong management, upward revenue and earnings trends, and large market opportunities.

In 1992, RedChip put coverage on what was then a small company in Seattle, called Starbucks. The stock was trading at $6.50 at the time of our coverage. RedChip was the first to put independent, nonbanking research on the stock.

Starbucks went public on June 26, 1992 at a price of $17 per share and closed trading that first day at $21.50 per share. We issued our coverage when the stock was a split adjusted $6.50. Those who bought at $6.50, if they held through today, would have a 12,247% gain. A $10,000 investment then would be worth $1.2 million today.

Buy When No One Is Paying Attention

That's exactly how the microcap pros make millions. They buy stocks before they get liquid, while they are quiet. They do their homework, find stocks that are truly undervalued in their peer group, and quietly begin accumulating. They are patient. They may be in a stock six months or three years before the Street finds out what they are missing. Take Q4, Quadrant Four Systems. I first had Dhru Desai on my show about four months ago. When this company signed with RedChip they were trading at six cents with very little volume. The stock reached a 52-week high of 66 cents within 4 months on November 29, 2013, a 1,000% gain. It then reached another 52-week high of $1.38 on December 9, 2013. A $10,000 investment at .06 cent would have been worth $230,000. But the stock did not hold that high, and at this point the stock is trading below 50 cents. Microcaps are the most volatile asset class. Imagine that.

The Misbehavior of Markets

The following was taken from the book, *The Misbehavior of Markets*, by Benoit B. Mandelbrot, whose thesis is that markets are not efficient, that there are too many factors that cannot be accounted for by financial models, which cause stocks to trade inefficently.

> *Shortly after the P/E factor was studied, economists discovered the January effect, a clear tendency of the market to rally every January. Then, a "small-firm effect" was discovered: portfolios of small company stocks outperformed large companies by 4.2 percent, economists found. And, further study found, a "small-firm-in-January effect," combining the two phenomena, was even more pronounced than either on its own.*

Mandelbrot argues convincingly that many trading strategies are not rooted in the realities of the market and neither are many financial models used to manage risk.

Map Your Course

It's important when investing in small-caps to establish guidelines for purchasing and selling your positions. It's also extremely important to be aware of some of the common dangers that you'll face. First, don't become too attached or emotional with any position. Second, don't try to time the market by buying at the lows and selling at the highs—you'll never succeed at this in the long term. Third, do your homework and don't depend on others to determine what's in your portfolio. If a position is keeping you up at night, is it worth it? Finally, don't worry about volatility. Ignore the market fluctuations and ask yourself if the reason you bought the stock in the first place still holds true. If it does, those fluctuations may present great opportunities to accumulate more shares at a lower cost. A current example of this last point would be the recent volatility experienced by Cancer Genetics (NASDAQ: CGIX). Currently trading below its October offering price of $14, CGIX represents a highly compelling opportunity.

Understand and Reduce Your Risk

Most investors don't take much time gaining the knowledge needed to understand a company before buying into it. Much like buying a lottery ticket with a dream about making money, investors often are tempted and buy on a whim or an impulse because they heard or read about a newly discovered technology or a company that plans to disrupt the industry. Take your time and understand everything you can about a company, and when the emotions wear-off then place your buy order. Take your time and study a company well and you'll increase your odds of success.

Microcap Indexes

FIGURE D.1 Dow Jones Select Microcap Index 10-Year: The Dow Jones Select Microcap (DJSM) Index measures the performance of microcaps trading on the major exchanges. Over a 10-year period it gained 100% compared to the S&P 500 & DJIA, which returned 83% and 72% respectively.

Data Source: Thomson Reuters Corporation.

FIGURE D.2 Dow Jones Select Microcap Index 5-Year: Over a 5-year period, the DJSM Index returned 107% compared to 104% and 88% for the S&P 500 and DJIA, respectively.
Data Source: Thomson Reuters Corporation.

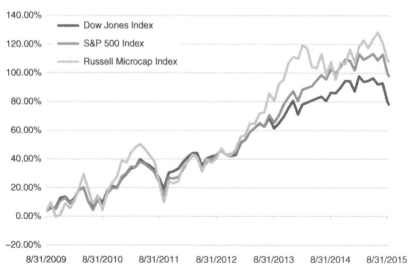

FIGURE D.3 Russell Microcap Index 5-Year: The Russell Microcap Index measures microcap performance. Over a 5-year period, it returned 112% compared to 103% and 89% for the S&P 500 and DJIA, respectively.
Data Source: Thomson Reuters Corporation.

166

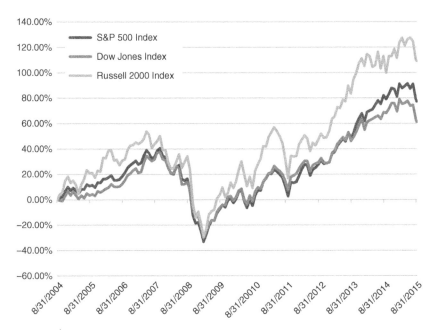

FIGURE D.4 Russell 2000 Index 10-Year: The Russell 2000 Index represents
the small-cap segment of equities. Over a 10-year period, it returned 115%
compared to 83% for the S&P 500 and 72% for the DJIA.
Data Source: Thomson Reuters Corporation.

Glossary of Wall Street Terms

10-K   An annual report summarizing a company's performance that must be submitted to the SEC within 60 days of the end of the fiscal year.

10-Q   A quarterly report submitted to the SEC that discloses information on a company's performance and financial position. It must be filed within 35 days of the first three fiscal quarters.

8-K   A report submitted to the SEC in order to disclose any unscheduled corporate changes or significant events that may be relevant to shareholders or have an influence on the value of the company's stock.

Bid Price versus Ask Price   Bid price indicates the maximum price buyers are willing to pay, while ask price is representative of the minimum price that a seller is willing to receive.

Big-Caps   Commonly referred to as "large caps," the term big-cap is used to describe any company with a market capitalization value above $10 billion. These are typically the primary players and blue-chip companies of the finance universe.

Blue Chip   The stock of a company that is recognized as reliable, well-established, and financially secure with an extensive record of stable growth. Typically these are large-cap companies with well-known products and services.

Blue Sky Laws   A set of securities laws unique to each state that aim to protect investors against fraudulent practices.

Bottom-Up Investment Approach   Investing based on the merit of a particular company or security with less attention granted to the industry or economy in which the company operates.

Broker-Dealer   An individual or firm that trades on its own account but also executes trades on behalf of clients.

Dow Jones   Dow Jones Industrial Average, a commonly watched stock market index that follows 30 large publicly traded companies.

FINRA   Financial Industry Regulatory Authority, a regulatory body responsible for monitoring business between brokers, dealers, and investors.

Float   Money in the banking system that is briefly counted twice due to delays in processing checks. Float is created when a bank credits a customer's account as soon as a check is deposited. However, it takes some time for the check to be received from the payer's bank. Until the check clears from the payer's bank, the amount of the check appears in the accounts of both the recipient's and payer's banks.

Fundamental Investor   An investor who evaluates a security based on a variety of objective and subjective factors in order to determine the security's intrinsic value and compare it to the current price.

GARP   Growth at a reasonable price, a method of investing in which companies with consistent earnings growth above broad market levels are targeted but companies with high valuations are disregarded.

Hedge Fund   An investment partnership between a fund manager and investors in which advanced and aggressive investment strategies are employed in order to generate high returns.

Index Funds   A type of mutual fund in which the portfolio is designed to follow a particular market index or list of stocks.

Insider Buying   Occurs when an individual employed by a publicly traded company purchases shares of the employer's stock based on public information.

Insider Trading Rules   Rules designed and enforced by the SEC in order to prevent individuals with inside information from gaining a distinct advantage over the investing public. Insider trading is illegal when trades are conducted before relevant company information has been made public. All insider trading must be reported to the SEC.

Institutional Buying   Purchasing securities in such large quantities or dollar amounts that preferential treatment and lower commissions are granted.

Investment Bank   A bank that facilitates trading by purchasing securities and selling them to the investing public. Investment banks also provide a variety of financial services such as facilitating mergers and underwriting.

IPO   Initial public offering, a process by which a private company becomes a public company. It is the first time that shares of stock in a company are sold to the general public.

Market Maker   A broker or firm that facilitates trading by holding inventory of a particular security and competing for customer orders.

Microcaps   A company with a market capitalization value between $50 million and $300 million.

Mid-Caps   Refers to any company with a market capitalization value between $2 billion and $10 billion.

Mutual Funds   A collection of funds that are invested in securities by a money manager who constructs a diversified portfolio based on the objectives of investors.

Nano-Caps   Popularly referred to as "penny stocks," nano-caps include any publicly traded company with a market capitalization value that falls below $50 million.

NASDAQ   National Association of Securities Dealers Automated Quotations, an electronic marketplace founded in 1971.

NYSE   Often referred to as the "Big Board," the NYSE is the oldest U.S. stock exchange, located on Wall Street in New York City. NYSE is one of the few remaining financial markets to use a physical trading floor to conduct trading. Representatives of buyers and sellers meet and shout prices in an open-outcry system.

NYSE MKT   Formerly known as the American Stock Exchange or AMEX, this is the third-largest stock exchange by volume in the United States. Trading in this market is almost exclusively concerned with small-cap stocks.

Outstanding Shares   A company's stock currently held by all its shareholders, including share blocks held by institutional investors and restricted shares owned by the company's officers and insiders. Outstanding shares are shown on a company's balance sheet under the heading "Capital Stock." The number of outstanding shares is used in calculating key metrics such as a company's market capitalization, as well as its earnings per share (EPS) and cash flow per share (CFPS).

PIPE   Private investment in a public equity, typically refers to an equity raise done by a publicly traded company with institutional and high-net-worth investors.

Quantitative Investment Approach   Investing based on mathematical factors and numerical methods of analysis while disregarding subjective criteria such as management profiles and brand-name recognition.

Reg FD   Regulation fair disclosure, a rule adopted by the SEC on August 15, 2000, that requires a public disclosure of any information provided to shareholders or market professionals.

Registered Direct   A registered direct offering is a public offering that is sold by a placement agent on an agency, or best efforts, basis (rather than a firm commitment underwriting). A registered direct offering is marketed and sold much like a PIPE (private investment in public equity) transaction to a selected number of accredited and institutional investors. However, since registered direct offerings are fully registered transactions, shares in those offerings can be sold to anyone. Because they can be marketed like PIPE offerings, registered direct offerings often are referred to as "registered PIPEs."

Reverse Mergers   Commonly referred to as "reverse takeover" or "reverse IPO," it enables private companies to become publicly traded by acquiring a majority of shares in a public company and then merging the two entities. This process is less complicated, less time consuming, and less expensive than a conventional IPO.

Russell 2000   A stock market index that is generally considered a benchmark for small-cap stocks, it measures approximately 2,000 companies as a sub-group of the Russell 3000.

Russell 3000   A stock market index weighted by market capitalization and includes the 3,000 largest U.S. equities.

S&P   Standard & Poor's 500, a commonly followed stock market index that is based on the market capitalizations of 500 large companies listed on the NASDAQ or NYSE.

SEC   Securities and Exchange Commission, a federal government entity charged with regulating the securities markets, monitoring corporate takeovers, and protecting investors from fraudulent business practices in the United States.

Secondary   Short for "secondary offering," refers to a public offering of newly issued stock from a company following their IPO.

Small-Caps   Typically refers to any company with a market capitalization between $300 million and $2 billion, though these parameters may vary among brokerages.

SPAC   Special-purpose acquisition company, also referred to as a "targeted acquisition company" (TAC), a SPAC raises money from the public with the intention of purchasing an existing private company.

Value Investor   An investor who targets companies that are believed to be undervalued by the general market.

Twenty-Five Financial and Business Books Worth Reading

1. *Against the Gods: The Remarkable Story of Risk*, Peter L. Bernstein
2. *The Misbehavior of Markets: A Fractal View of Risk, Ruin & Reward*, Benoit Mandelbrot and Richard L. Hudson
3. *Fooled by Randomness: The Hidden Role of Chance in Life and in the Markets*, Nassim Nicholas Taleb
4. *House of Cards: A Tale of Hubris and Wretched Excess on Wall Street*, William D. Cohan
5. *The Big Short*, Michael Lewis
6. *Bull: A History of the Boom and Bust, 1982–2004*, Maggie Mahar
7. *Money and Power: How Goldman Sachs Came to Rule the World*, William D. Cohan
8. *The Mind of Wall Street: A Legendary Financier on the Perils of Greed and the Mysteries of the Market*, Leon Levy
9. *Take on the Street: What Wall Street and Corporate America Don't Want You to Know*, Arthur Levitt
10. *While America Aged: How Pension Debts Ruined General Motors, Stopped the NYC Subways, Bankrupted San Diego, and Loom as the Next Financial Crisis*, Robert Lowenstein
11. *Origins of the Crash: The Great Bubble and Its Undoing*, Roger Lowenstein
12. *Bad Money: Reckless Finance, Failed Politics, and the Global Crisis of American Capitalism*, Kevin Phillips
13. *Griftopia: A Story of Bankers, Politicians, and the Most Audacious Power Grab in American History*, Matt Taibbi
14. *The Great Crash 1929*, John Kenneth Galbraith
15. *Super Money*, Adam Smith
16. *Indecent Exposure: A True Story of Hollywood and Wall Street*, David McClintick

17. *Secrets of the Street: The Dark Side of Making Money*, Gene G. Marcial
18. *Understanding Wall Street* (Fifth Edition), Jeffrey B. Little and Lucien Rhodes
19. *Biography of the Dollar: How the Mighty Buck Conquered the World and Why It's Under Siege*, Craig Karmin
20. *Eight Steps to Seven Figures: The Investment Strategies of Everyday Millionaires and How You Can Become Wealthy Too*, Charles B. Carlson, CFA
21. *Warren Buffett and the Interpretation of Financial Statements*, Mary Buffett and David Clark
22. *Think and Grow Rich*, Napoleon Hill
23. *The Very Very Rich and How They Got That Way*, Max Gunthers
24. *The Millionaire Mind*, Thomas J. Stanley, PhD
25. *The First Billion Is the Hardest*, T. Boone Pickens

About the Author

Dave Gentry has been a consultant to over 400 public and private companies. In 2012, he founded *The RedChip Money Report*™, a weekly cable TV financial news show broadcast in over 200 million homes on Fox Business, Bloomberg Europe, and Bloomberg Asia. He is the chief executive officer of RedChip Companies Inc., an international investor relations, media, and research firm focused on smaller-cap stocks. He has appeared as a guest on CNBC and Fox Business News, and is a nationally recognized thought leader in the microcap sector.

Index

Printed and bound by CPI Group (UK) Ltd, Croydon, CR0 4YY

13/04/2025

14656498-0001